2004

To Dylan from Grandma

PICTURE DICTIONARY

FRENCH-ENGLISH

FRENCH-ENGLISH PICTURE DICTIONARY

Copyright © 1990 Éditions Rényi Inc.

Illustrated by Kathryn Adams, Pat Gangnon, Colin Gillies, David Shaw and Yvonne Zan.
Designed by David Shaw and Associates.

Color separations by New Concept Limited

Printed in Canada by Metropole Litho Inc.

In this dictionary, as in reference works in general, no mention is made of patents, trademark rights, or other proprietary rights which may attach to certain words or entries. The absence of such mention, however, in no way implies that the words or entries in question are exempt from such rights.

English language editors: P. O'Brien-Hitching, R. LeBel, P. Rényi, K. C. Sheppard.

French editors: by Sophie Arthaud, René Le Bel, Gina Lepage, Pierre Rényi, Patrice Soulard

Originally published by Éditions Rényi Inc., Toronto, Canada

Distributed exclusively in trade and education in the United States of America by Langenscheidt Publishers, Inc., Maspeth, New York 11378

Hardcover ISBN 0-88729-851-6
Softcover ISBN 0-88729-857-5

Distributed outside the USA by Éditions Rényi Inc., Toronto, Canada

Hardcover ISBN 0-921606-02-8
Softcover ISBN 0-921606-47-8

INTRODUCTION

Some of Canada's best illustrators have contributed to this Picture Dictionary, which has been carefully designed to combine words and pictures into a pleasurable learning experience.

Its unusually large number of terms (3336) makes this Picture Dictionary a flexible teaching tool. It is excellent for helping young children acquire language and dictionary skills. Because the vocabulary it encompasses is so broad, this dictionary can also be used to teach new words to older children and adults as well. Further, it is also an effective tool for teaching English as a second language.

THE VOCABULARY

The decision on which words to include and which to leave out was made in relation to three standards. First, a word-frequency analysis was carried out to include the most common words. Then a thematic clustering analysis was done to make sure that words in common themes (animals, plants, activities etc.) were included. Finally, the vocabulary was expanded to include words which children would likely hear, ask about and use. This makes this dictionary's vocabulary more honest than most. 'To choke', 'greedy', 'to smoke' are included, but approval is withheld.

This process was further complicated by the decision to *systematically* illustrate the meanings. Although the degree of abstraction was kept reasonably low, it was considered necessary to include terms such as 'to expect' and 'to forgive', which are virtually impossible to illustrate. Instead of dropping these terms, we decided to provide explanatory sentences that create a context.

Where variations occur between British and North American English, both terms are given, with an asterisk marking the British version (favor/favour*, gas/petrol*).

USING THIS DICTIONARY

Used at home, this dictionary is an enjoyable book for children to explore alone or with their parents. The pictures excite the imagination of younger children and entice them to ask questions. Older children in televisual cultures often look to visual imagery as an aid to meaning. The pictures help them make the transition from the graphic to the written. Even young adults will find the book useful, because the illustrations, while amusing, are not childish.

The dictionary as a whole provides an occasion to introduce students to basic dictionary skills. This work is compatible with school reading materials in current use, and can serve as a 'user-friendly' reference tool.

Great care has been taken to ensure that any contextual statements made are factual, have some educational value and are compatible with statements made elsewhere in the book. Lastly, from a strictly pedagogical viewpoint, the little girl featured in the book has not been made into a paragon of virtue; young users will readily identify with her imperfections.

À TOUS MES NOUVEAUX AMIS

Je m'appelle Julie. Je vais à l'école. J'apprends à nager. J'ai un petit frère et mille idées. Si tu veux rencontrer mon papa, qui est amiral, regarde à droite au bas de la page. Maman est à la page suivante, en haut. Pour faire ma connaissance, rends-toi directement au mot ''calme''.

Les gens pensent parfois que les dictionnaires sont des livres ennuyeux. C'est sans doute qu'ils n'ont jamais vu celui-ci, qui parle de moi, de ma famille et de mes amis.

Cinq grandes personnes se sont beaucoup amusées à faire les illustrations. Moi, j'ai dessiné une image, celle du zèbre : essaie de la trouver!

Je dois te quitter maintenant. Mais tu me retrouveras, page après page.

le boulier

1   abacus

de, environ, autour de

Parle-moi **de** cela.
Cela prend **environ**
une heure.
Jacques regarde
autour de lui.

Tell me about it.
It takes about an hour.
Jacques looks about him.

2   about

La pomme est **au-dessus**
de sa tête.

3   above

Paul est **absent** aujourd'hui.

4   absent

Toutes les autos ont
un accélérateur.

5   accelerator

un accent

John a **un accent**
britannique.
Mets **l'accent** sur la
première syllabe.

John has a British accent.
Put the accent on the first
syllable.

6   accent

un accident

7   accident

un accordéon

8   accordion

On **a accusé** Sophie.

9   to accuse

un as de pique

10   ace

J'ai mal à la tête.

11   My head aches.

Un acide peut brûler la peau.

12   acid

Le gland est le fruit du chêne.

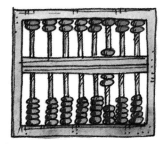

13   acorn

une acrobate

14   acrobat

de l'autre côté, à travers

Paul habite **de l'autre côté**
de la rue.
Alice court **à travers**
champs.

Paul lives across the street.
Alice runs across the fields.

15   across

additionner

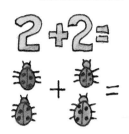

16   to add

C'est **l'adresse** de Julie.

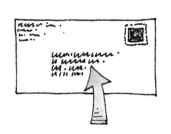

17   address

Le papa de Julie est **amiral.**

18   admiral

Bertrand **adore** Claire.

19   to adore

Un adulte est
une grande personne.

20   adult

Avance ton roi!

21   to advance

Barnabé a **l'avantage**.

22   advantage

La maman de Julie aime
l'aventure.

23   adventure

Philippe **a peur.**

24   He is afraid..

L'Afrique est un continent.

25   Africa

après

Tu peux jouer **après** le dîner.
Répète **après** moi!
Cours **après** la balle!

You can play after dinner.
Repeat after me!
Run after the ball!

26   after

L'après-midi
commence à 12 heures.

27   afternoon

encore, de nouveau

Joue **encore** ce morceau!
C'est ton tour **de nouveau.**

Play it again!
It is your turn again.

28   again

Minou se frotte **contre**
les jambes de François.

29   to rub **against**

Quelle différence d'**âge**!

30   age

une personne **agile**

31   agile person

Le bateau **s'est échoué.**

32   aground

devant, à l'avance

Hélène est assise
devant Pierre.
Planifie tes vacances
à l'avance!

Hélène sits ahead of Pierre.
Plan ahead for your
holidays!

33   ahead

porter **secours**

34   to provide **aid**

Est-ce qu'elle **vise** bien la cible?

35   to aim

Le cerf-volant plane dans **l'air.**

36   air

Zénon dort sur
le matelas pneumatique.

37   air mattress

un insecte dans un vase
hermétique

38   airtight

Cet **avion** semble en difficulté.

39   airplane/aeroplane*

Les avions atterrissent à l'**aéroport**.	**une allée, un couloir**	le réveil, le réveille-matin	**un album de photos**
40 airport	41 aisle	42 alarm clock	43 album
La maison est **en feu**.	L'un des deux poissons est bien **vivant**.	Je les veux **tous**.	un chat dans **la ruelle**
44 alight	45 alive	46 I want them **all**.	47 alley
un alligator	**une amande**	Milou peut **presque** attraper l'os.	Pourquoi est-il **seul**?
48 alligator	49 almond	50 almost	51 alone
Nous marchons **le long de** la rivière.	**à haute voix**	**un alphabet** A B C D E F G H I J K L M N O P Q R S T U V W X Y Z a b c d e f g h i j k l m n o p q r s t u v w x y z	Est-ce que je dois **déjà** partir?
52 along	53 aloud	54 alphabet	55 Do I have to go **already**?
Je n'ai **pas de mal**, ça va.	J'en veux **aussi**.	une échelle en **aluminium**	Je tombe **toujours**.
56 I am **alright**.	57 I **also** want some.	58 aluminum/aluminium* ladder	59 I **always** fall down.

une ambulance	un loup **parmi** les moutons	**une ancre**	des ruines **anciennes**
60 ambulance	61 wolf **among** sheep	62 anchor	63 ancient
un angle	Il est **fâché**.	**les animaux**	**la cheville**
64 angle	65 He is **angry**.	66 animals	67 ankle
annoncer	un **autre** sandwich	**La réponse** est...	**la fourmi**
68 to announce	69 **another** sandwich	70 The **answer** is...	71 ant
L'Antarctique	**une antilope**	**les bois** de l'élan	Je **n'ai pas** d'argent.
72 Antarctic	73 antelope	74 antlers	75 I do not have **any** money.
Ça mange **de tout**.	Il ne peut aller **nulle part**.	**à part, séparé**	**le singe**
76 It eats **anything**.	77 He cannot go **anywhere**.	78 apart	79 ape

la ruche des abeilles

80 apiary

faire ses excuses, excuser

Faire ses excuses, c'est demander pardon.
Excusez-moi d'être en retard!

To apologize means to say you are sorry.
I apologize for being late!

81 to apologize/apologise*

apparaître

Le magicien a fait apparaître un lapin.
Le soleil apparaît à l'horizon.

The magician made a rabbit appear.
The sun appears on the horizon.

82 to appear

applaudir

83 to applaud

la pomme

84 apple

le trognon de pomme

85 apple core

approcher

86 to approach

un abricot

87 apricot

En avril, ne te découvre pas d'un fil!

88 April

le tablier

89 apron

un aquarium

90 aquarium

une arche

91 arch

un architecte

92 architect

Il fait un froid glacial dans l'Arctique.

93 Arctic

discuter, se disputer

94 to argue

le bras

95 arm

le fauteuil

96 armchair

Le chevalier porte une armure.

97 armor/armour*

une aisselle

98 armpit

autour, environ, vers

Autour du monde en quatre-vingts jours
Un autobus pèse environ 6 tonnes.
Nous y serons vers midi.

Around the world in eighty days
A bus weighs around 6 tons.
We will be there around noon.

99 around

arranger des fleurs

100   to **arrange** flowers

Le policier **arrête** Jules.

101   to **arrest**

---

arriver

102   to **arrive**

---

la flèche

103   arrow

---

un artichaut

104   artichoke

---

un artiste

105   artist

---

aussi, comme

Toto est **aussi** grand
que Patrice.
Le petit frère de Paul est
beau **comme** un coeur!

*Toto is as tall as Patrice.
Paul's little brother is really
cute!*

106   as

---

la cendre

107   ash

---

le cendrier

108   ashtray

L'Asie est un continent.

109   Asia

---

demander son chemin

110   to **ask** for directions

Marie et son chat sont
tous deux **endormis**.

111   asleep

---

les asperges

112   asparagus

Il lui faudra peut-être
deux **aspirines**.

113   aspirin

Patrick **a étonné** Jeanne.

114   to **astonish**

---

un astronaute

115   astronaut

---

un astronome

116   astronomer

à, au

Hélène est **à** la maison
avec son papa.
Ils regardent le tableau.
Va **au** lit tout de suite!

*Hélène is at home with
her father.
They are looking at
the picture.
Go to bed at once!*

117   at

---

une athlète

118   athlete

---

un atlas

119   atlas

l'atmosphère de la terre 120 atmosphere	**un atome** 121 atom	**attacher** 122 to attach	Fais **attention!** 123 Pay attention!
le grenier 124 attic	**un auditoire** 125 audience	**Août** est le huitième mois de l'année. 126 August	Ma **tante** est la sœur de ma mère. 127 My **aunt** is my mother's sister.
L'Australie est la plus grande île du monde. 128 Australia	**un auteur** 129 author	un réveil **automatique** 130 automatic	**L'automne** est l'une des quatre saisons. 131 autumn
une avalanche 132 avalanche	**un avocat** 133 avocado	Pourquoi Jules reste-t-il **éveillé?** 134 awake	Elle est **partie.** 135 She is away.
une **affreuse** odeur 136 an awful smell	une personne **maladroite** 137 an awkward person	**une hache** 138 axe	**Un essieu** relie deux roues. 139 axle

B

le bébé

140   baby

la voiture d'enfant

141   baby carriage/pram*

Gratte-moi **le dos**!

142   back

des œufs au **lard**

144   bacon and eggs

Cette pomme est **mauvaise**.

145   bad apple

un insigne

146   badge

reculer

143   to back up

Qu'est-ce qu'il y a dans **le sac**?

147   bag

un appât à souris

148   bait

cuire, faire cuire

149   to bake

Le boulanger cuit du pain.

150   baker

la boulangerie

151   bakery

L'acrobate est bien en **équilibre** sur la corde.

152   good balance

le balcon

153   balcony

Pierrot est **chauve**.

154   bald

la balle

155   ball

la ballerine

156   ballerina

le ballet

157   ballet

le ballon

158   balloon

la montgolfière

159   hot air **balloon**

la banane

160   banana

le bandeau

161   band

un orchestre

162   musical **band**

Le pansement fait du bien à Michel.

163   bandage

frapper

164   to bang

Michel descend l'escalier sur **la rampe**.

165   banister

Michel porte son argent à **la banque**.

166   bank

la barre

167   bar

Les bars sont réservés aux adultes.

168   bar/pub*

le fil de fer barbelé

169   barbed wire

Le coiffeur lui coupe les cheveux.

170   barber

un pied **nu**

171   one **bare** foot

une aubaine, des soldes

172   bargain

la péniche

173   barge

aboyer

174   to bark

L'orge pousse dans les champs.

176   barley

la grange

177   barn

la caserne des soldats

178   barracks

une écorce

175   bark

le tonneau, la barrique

179   barrel

le canon du revolver

180   barrel

la barrette

181   barrette/hair slide*

la barrière

182   barrier

la base de la colonne

183   base

le but de base-ball

184   base

le base-ball

185   baseball

le sous-sol

186   basement/cellar*

le basilic

187   basil

le panier

188   basket

le basket-ball

189   basketball

les bâtons

190   bats

192   I am having a bath.

193   bathroom

194   bathtub

191   bat

une pile électrique
pour ta radio

195   battery

Le bateau navigue dans **la baie**.

196   bay

Maman épice le ragoût avec
des feuilles de **laurier**.

197   bay leaves

le bazar

198   bazaar

être

Promets-moi d'**être** gentil!
Antoine **est** très intelligent.
Roméo et Juliette
sont amoureux.

Promise me that you
will be good!
Antoine is very intelligent.
Romeo and Juliet are in love.

199 to be

la plage

200 beach

la perle

201 bead

le bec

202 beak

le faisceau de lumière

203 beam of light

les haricots, les fèves

204 beans

L'ours fait du vélo.

205 bear

Pépé a **une** longue **barbe**.

206 beard

Quelle horrible **bête!**

207 beast

Paulette **bat** le tambour.

208 to beat

Fifi est **belle!**

209 beautiful

le castor

210 beaver

Je pleure **parce que...**

211 I am crying because...

devenir

La chenille

devient

papillon.

212 to become

le lit

213 bed

la lampe de chevet

214 bed lamp/reading light*

la chambre à coucher

215 bedroom

L'abeille est un insecte utile.

216 bee

un hêtre

217 beech

Les abeilles vivent
dans **la ruche.**

218 beehive

une chope de **bière**

219   beer

la betterave

220   beet/beetroot*

le scarabée

221   beetle

Lave-toi les mains **avant** le dîner!

222   Wash your hands **before** dinner.

mendier

223   to beg

commencer

Pour **commencer**, prenons le petit déjeuner.
La leçon de piano de Julie **commence** à dix heures.

To begin with,
let's have breakfast.
Julie's piano lesson begins at ten o'clock.

224   to begin

Alice **se conduit bien**.

225   to behave

Noémie se cache **derrière** l'arbre.

226   behind

beige

227   beige

Je **crois** aux dragons.

228   I **believe** in dragons.

la cloche, la clochette

229   bell

le nombril

230   belly button

Il m'**appartient**.

231   He **belongs** to me.

Le chat est **en dessous** de la table.

232   below

la ceinture

233   belt

le banc

234   bench

le tournant de la route

235   bend

plier, tordre

236   to bend

Marcel porte **un béret**.

237   beret

Patricia est **à côté** de l'arbre.

238   beside

autre, d'ailleurs

Ne crois-tu pas que tu devrais manger **autre** chose que du dessert?
D'ailleurs, tu ne devrais pas manger tant de sucre.

Should you not eat something else besides dessert?
Besides, you should not eat so much sugar.

239   besides

la meilleure

240   best

mieux, meilleur

Julie écrit **mieux** que David.
Les fruits sont **meilleurs** que le chocolat.

Julie writes better than David.
Fruit is better than chocolate.

241   better

Philippe marche **entre** les rochers.

242   between

le bavoir

243   bib

la bicyclette, le vélo

244   bicycle

grand

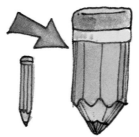

245   big

Le vélo de Philippe a un guidon de course.

246   bike

le billet

247   bill/banknote*

le panneau d'affichage

248   billboard/hoarding*

le jeu de billard

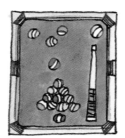

249   billiards/snooker*

attacher

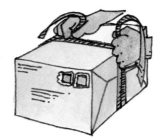

250   to bind/tie up*

les jumelles

251   binoculars

un oiseau

252   bird

la naissance

Julie pesait sept livres à **la naissance**.
La chatte a donné **naissance** à quatre petits chatons.

Julie weighed seven pounds at birth.
The cat gave birth to four little kittens.

253   birth

Bon **anniversaire**!

254   birthday

le biscuit

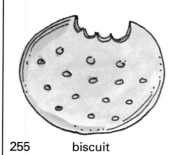

255   biscuit

Frédéric **mord** à belles dents dans son sandwich.

256   to bite

la bouchée, la morsure

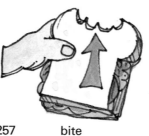

257   bite

amer

La bière a un goût **amer.**
Julie a versé des larmes **amères** quand elle a perdu sa poupée.

Beer has a bitter taste.
Julie wept bitter tears when she lost her doll.

258   bitter

noir  259 black	**la mûre** 260 blackberry	**le merle** 261 blackbird	**le tableau noir** 262 blackboard

le cassis 263 blackcurrant	**le forgeron** 264 blacksmith	**la lame** de l'épée 265 blade	**blâmer, reprocher** Papa **a reproché** à Julie d'avoir cassé le vase, mais elle est innocente. C'est David que Papa devrait **blâmer**! *Father blamed Julie for breaking the vase, but she did not do it. Father should blame David!* 266 to blame

la page vierge 267 blank page	**la couverture** 268 blanket	**Une explosion** fait un bruit de tonnerre. 269 blast	**faire sauter** 270 to blast

le feu, l'incendie 271 blaze	**le veston, le blazer** 272 blazer	**L'eau de javel** sert à blanchir le linge. 273 bleach	Elle **saigne** du nez. 274 to bleed

le mélangeur 275 blender	**un aveugle** 276 blind	**cligner des yeux** 277 to blink	**Une ampoule,** ça fait mal! 278 blister

la tempête de neige

279   blizzard

le cube

280   block

le pâté de maisons

281   block

Le policier lui **bloque** le chemin.

282   to block

les cheveux **blonds**

283   blond/blonde*

une transfusion de **sang**

284   blood

la floraison

285   bloom

Au printemps, les arbres **fleurissent.**

286   to blossom

une grosse **tache** d'encre

287   blot

la blouse, le chemisier

288   blouse

un coup sur la tête

289   a **blow** to the head

souffler

290   to **blow**

bleu

291   blue

la myrtille, le bleuet

292   blueberries

émoussé

La lame du couteau est trop **émoussée** pour couper la tomate.
Alice n'a pas ménagé ses mots avec lui!

The blade of the knife is too blunt to cut the tomato. Alice was very blunt with him.

293   blunt

Caroline **rougit** facilement.

294   to blush

le sanglier

295   boar

la planche

296   board

se vanter

Christophe **se vante** tout le temps.
Il ne peut pas **se vanter** d'être modeste!

*Christophe is always boasting.
His modesty is nothing to boast about!*

297   to boast

le canot, la barque

298   boat

une épingle à cheveux

299   bobby pin/hairgrip*

le corps humain

300   body

bouillir

301   to boil

le boulon

302   bolt

un os pour le chien

303   bone

le feu de joie

304   bonfire

le livre

305   book

une étagère à livres

306   bookshelf

le boomerang

307   boomerang

la botte

308   boot

la frontière entre deux pays

309   border

C'est dur de percer un trou dans du béton!

310   to bore

né

En quelle année es-tu **né**?
C'est un meneur-**né**.

What year were you born?
He is a born leader.

312   born

emprunter

Julie **emprunte** souvent
la bicyclette de son frère.

Julie often borrows her
brother's bike.

313   to borrow

le patron

314   boss

ennuyer

Julie **ennuie** parfois
les gens à en mourir!
Robert m'**ennuie** avec
toutes ses paroles.

Julie can bore people
to death!
Robert bores me because
he talks too much.

311   to bore

tous deux

Natalie et Mathieu sont
tous deux mignons.
Tous deux ont un gentil
sourire.

Natalie and Mathieu are
both cute.
Both have a nice smile.

315   both

la bouteille

316   bottle

un ouvre-bouteille, un décapsuleur

317   bottle opener

le fond de l'aquarium

318   bottom

un gros caillou

319   boulder

Le ballon **rebondit**.

320   to bounce

un bouquet de fleurs

321   bouquet

un arc et des flèches

322   bow

le bol

324   bowl

Y a-t-il quelque chose dans **la boîte?**

325   box

le boxeur

326   boxer

le nœud papillon

323   bow tie

le garçon

327   boy

le soutien-gorge

328   bra

le bracelet

329   bracelet

se vanter

Noémie **se vante** d'avoir beaucoup de jouets.
Son papa lui dit de ne pas **se vanter**.

Noémie brags about the number of toys she has. Her father tells her not to brag.

330   to brag

le cerveau

331   brain

Pour arrêter la voiture, on utilise **les freins**.

332   brake

freiner

333   to brake

la branche de l'arbre

334   branch

courageux

Le dentiste dit que tu as été très **courageuse**, Julie.

The dentist says you were very brave, Julie.

335   brave

le pain

336   bread

La lampe **est cassée**.

337   to break

La voiture est **en panne**.

338   to break down

Le voleur **est entré par effraction.**

339   to break in

le petit déjeuner

340   breakfast

Le dragon a mauvaise **haleine.**

341   breath

respirer

342   to breathe

la brique

343   brick

Le maçon construit un mur de briques.

344   bricklayer

La mariée est un peu timide.

345   bride

Le marié aussi.

346   bridegroom

le pont

347   bridge

la bride du cheval

348   bridle

la serviette

349   briefcase

un soleil **éclatant**

350   bright sun

Milou **apporte** les pantoufles.

351   to bring

Julie **rapporte** les livres à la bibliothèque.

352   to bring back

un verre **cassant**

353   brittle glass

le brocoli

354   broccoli

la broche

355   brooch

Le ruisseau court à travers champs.

356   brook

le balai

357   broom

J'aime mon **frère.**

358   I love my brother.

le sourcil

359   brow

brun

360   brown

Martin a besoin de se **brosser** les cheveux.

362   to brush

la brosse

363   brush

Mathieu a **un bleu** au bras.

361   bruise

des choux de Bruxelles

366   brussels sprouts

le pinceau

364   paintbrush

la brosse à dents

365   toothbrush

Brigitte aime les bains pleins de **bulles**.

367   bubble

le seau

368   bucket

la boucle d'une ceinture

369   belt buckle

le bourgeon

370   bud

le bison

371   buffalo

un insecte

372   bug

le clairon du soldat

373   bugle

construire

374   to build

le taureau

375   bull

le bulldozer

376   bulldozer

Les balles de fusil sont dangereuses.

377   bullet

le porte-voix

378   bullhorn/megaphone*

Cet homme est une brute.

379   bully

Laurent a une bosse sur la tête.

380   bump

les pare-chocs

381   bumpers

la botte d'asperges

382   bunch

le fagot de bois

383   bundle

la bouée

384   buoy

le cambrioleur

385   burglar

Le feu brûle dans l'âtre.

386   to burn

Boum! Le ballon éclate.

387   to burst

enterrer

388   to bury

un autobus

389   bus

un arrêt d'autobus

390   bus stop

Un arbuste est plus petit qu'un   arbre.

391   bush

Pas maintenant, je suis occupé.

392   I am busy now.

mais

Je voudrais bien venir, **mais** je suis occupé.
Paul est grand, **mais** sa soeur est plus grande encore.

I would like to come, but I am busy.
Paul is big, but his sister is bigger.

393   but

le boucher

394   butcher

le beurre

395   butter

le papillon

396   butterfly

les boutons

397   buttons

Philippe achète une crème glacée.

398   to buy

le chou

399   cabbage

la cabane dans la forêt

400   cabin

une armoire

401   cabinet

le câble

402   cable/lead*

le cactus

403   cactus

la cage

404   cage

le gâteau

405   cake

la calculatrice

406   calculator

le calendrier

407   calendar

Le veau est le petit de la vache.

408   calf

appeler

409   to call

Julie est toujours **calme**.

412   She is **calm**.

le chameau

413   camel

un appareil-photo

414   camera

annuler

Nous **annulerons** le pique-nique s'il pleut.
Julie **a annulé** notre visite au zoo.

We will call off the picnic if it rains.
Julie has called off our trip to the zoo.

410   to **call off**

Lucie et France **campent** sous la tente.

415   to camp

le campement

416   campsite

la boîte

417   can

téléphoner

411   to **call up**/to **phone***

un ouvre-boîte

418 can opener/tin* opener

Le bateau vogue sur **le canal**.

419   canal

le canari

420   canary

la bougie

421   candle

le chandelier

422   candlestick

les bonbons

423   candy/sweets*

Il marche avec **une canne**.

424   cane/walking stick*

le canon

425   cannon

Je **ne peux pas** voir.

426   I cannot see.

le canot, le canoë

427   canoe

le cantaloup

428   cantaloupe

La rivière serpente dans **le canyon**.

429   canyon

la casquette

430   cap

le cap

431   cape

la cape

432   cape

une lettre **majuscule**

433   capital

le capitaine du bateau

434   captain

capturer un papillon

435   to capture

la voiture

436   car

La caravane traverse le désert.

437   caravan

les cartes

438   cards

la boîte en carton

439   cardboard

L'infirmière **soigne** les malades.

440   to care

Sébastien est **insouciant**.

441   He is careless.

la cargaison d'un avion

442   cargo

un œillet

443   carnation

le carnaval

444   carnival

le charpentier

445   carpenter

le tapis

446   carpet

la voiture d'enfant

447   carriage/pram*

la carotte

448   carrot

Le déménageur **porte** une grosse caisse.

449   to carry

la charrette

450   cart

Les vis sont rangées dans **le carton**.

451   carton

découper une tranche de poulet

452   to carve

le coffre

453   case

de l'argent liquide

454   cash

des noix d'acajou

455   cashew nuts

le château

456   castle

le chat

457   cat

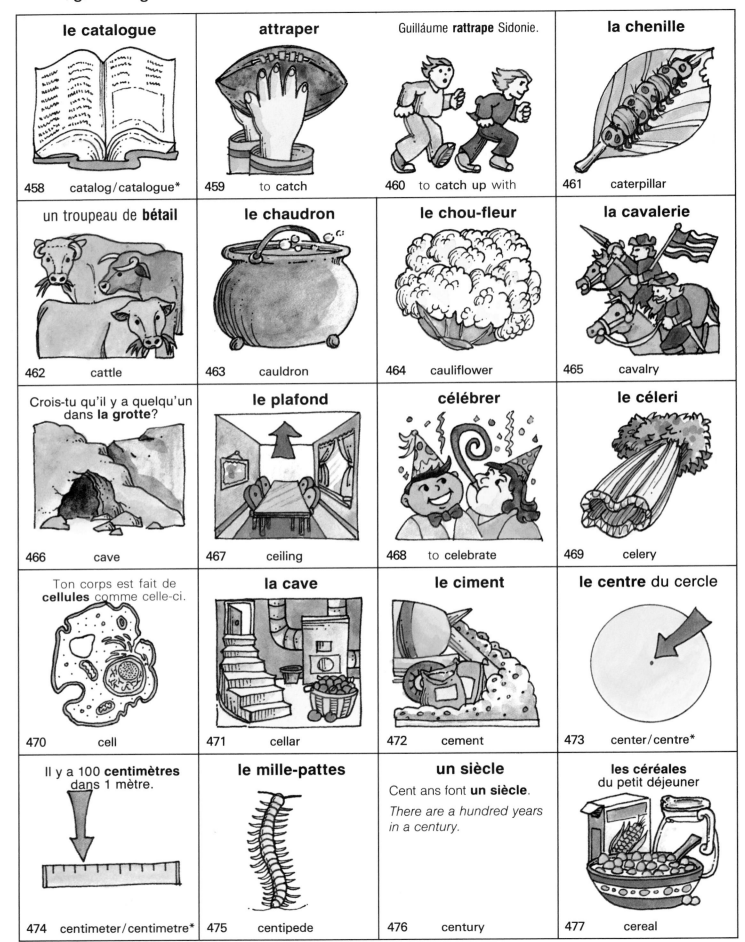

le catalogue

458   catalog/catalogue*

attraper

459   to catch

Guilláume **rattrape** Sidonie.

460   to **catch up** with

la chenille

461   caterpillar

un troupeau de **bétail**

462   cattle

le chaudron

463   cauldron

le chou-fleur

464   cauliflower

la cavalerie

465   cavalry

Crois-tu qu'il y a quelqu'un dans **la grotte**?

466   cave

le plafond

467   ceiling

célébrer

468   to celebrate

le céleri

469   celery

Ton corps est fait de **cellules** comme celle-ci.

470   cell

la cave

471   cellar

le ciment

472   cement

le centre du cercle

473   center/centre*

Il y a 100 **centimètres** dans 1 mètre.

474   centimeter/centimetre*

le mille-pattes

475   centipede

un siècle

Cent ans font **un siècle**.

There are a hundred years in a century.

476   century

les céréales du petit déjeuner

477   cereal

certain

Julie est **certaine**
d'avoir raison.
Elle a **certains** sentiments
pour Laurent.

*Julie is certain that she
is right.*
*She has a certain feeling
about Laurent.*

478   certain

le certificat

479   certificate

la chaîne

480   chain

la tronçonneuse

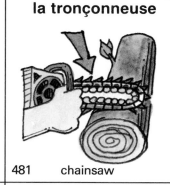

481   chainsaw

la chaise

482   chair

la craie

483   chalk

la championne

484   champion

la monnaie

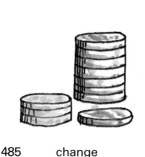

485   change

le chenal, le canal

487   channel

le douzième **chapitre** du livre

488   chapter

le caractère

Julie a du **caractère**.
Que veut dire ce **caractère**
chinois?

*Julie has a strong
character.*
*What does this Chinese
character mean?*

489   character

changer, se changer

486   to change

le charbon de bois

490   charcoal

le cardon

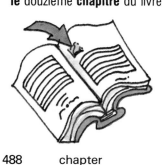

491   chard

inculper, recharger

La police **a inculpé** Jules
de vol.
Ton jouet s'est arrêté parce
que j'ai oublié de **recharger**
la batterie.

*The police charged Jules
with robbery.*
*Your toy has stopped
because I forgot to charge
the battery.*

492   to charge

le char-

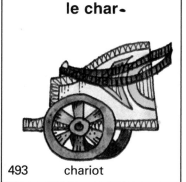

493   chariot

le graphique

494   chart

poursuivre

495   to chase

bavarder

496   to chat

un crayon **bon marché**, une couronne chère

497   cheap pencil, expensive crown

Éric essaie de **tricher**. 498 to cheat	**vérifier** As-tu **vérifié** ta montre ce matin? *Did you check your watch this morning?* 499 to check	**la joue** 500 cheek	**Le fromage** est fait avec du lait. 501 cheese
le chèque 502 cheque*/check	**les cerises** 503 cherries	**la poitrine** nue 504 chest	**les châtaignes, les marrons** 505 chestnut
Mâche bien avant d'avaler. 506 to chew	**les pois chiches** 507 chick peas	**le poulet** 508 chicken	Charles a **la varicelle**. 509 chicken-pox
Le chef salue les soldats. 510 chief	**l'enfant** 511 child	un jour **frais** 512 a chilly day	**la cheminée** 513 chimney
le chimpanzé 514 chimpanzee	**le menton** 515 chin	**la vaisselle** 516 china/crockery*	**un copeau** de bois 517 chip

le ciseau à bois du menuisier
518   chisel

la ciboulette
519   chives

le chocolat
520   chocolate

le chœur, la chorale
521   choir

Étrangler quelqu'un, ce n'est pas une blague.
522   to choke

Claude **s'étrangle** avec un os.
523   to choke on

Lequel des deux dois-je **choisir**?
524   to choose

hacher, couper
525   to chop

les baguettes
526   chopsticks

Le pare-choc de l'auto est **en chrome**.
527   chrome

le chrysanthème
528   chrysanthemum

le morceau de charbon
529   a chunk/lump* of coal

La fumée du **cigare** sent mauvais.
530   cigar

La cigarette est mauvaise pour la santé.
531   cigarette

le cercle
532   circle

le cirque
533   circus

Est-ce que tu vis dans **une** grande **ville?**
534   city

La palourde vit dans sa coquille.
535   clam

L'étau serre les deux planches ensemble.
536   clamp

applaudir
537   to clap

la classe

538 classroom

Le crabe a **des pinces** puissantes.

539 claw

---

l'argile

L'argile sert à faire des briques.
L'argile sert aussi à faire des pots.

Clay is used to make bricks.
Clay is also used for making pots.

540 clay

Elle est toute **propre**.

541 She is all **clean**.

Tante Annie **dessert** la table.

542 to clear

---

la falaise

543 cliff

---

grimper, escalader

544 to climb

---

la clinique

545 clinic

---

couper, tailler

546 to clip

---

une pendule

547 clock

Amandine **ferme** le livre.

548 to close

Ton **placard** est-il toujours bien rangé?

549 closet/cupboard*

---

le tissu, le linge

Les vêtements sont faits de **tissu**.
Maman se sert d'**un linge** à vaisselle pour essuyer les assiettes.

Clothes are made of cloth.
Mother uses a dishcloth to wipe the plates.

550 cloth

---

les vêtements

551 clothes

---

la corde à linge

552 clothes line

---

le nuage

553 cloud

Un trèfle à quatre feuilles porte bonheur.

554 clover

---

le clown

555 clown

Thal va à la chasse avec **une massue**.

556 club

---

l'indice, l'indication

La police a trouvé **un indice** dans cette affaire de vol.
Je vais te donner **une indication**.

The police found a clue to the robbery.
I will give you a clue.

557 clue

La pédale d'**embrayage** est tout à fait à gauche.

558   clutch

saisir, empoigner

559   to clutch

C'est notre **entraîneur**.

560   coach

Nous voyageons en **autocar**.

561   coach

Le charbon vient de la mine.

563   coal

rude, grossier

Cette étoffe est vraiment **rude**!
Ne sois pas **grossier**!

*This cloth is very coarse!
Do not use coarse
language!*

564   coarse

la côte

565   coast

entraîner

Martine **entraîne** notre équipe de volley-ball deux fois par semaine.

Martine coaches our volleyball team twice a week.

562   to coach

Tu as besoin d'**un manteau** chaud en hiver.

566   coat

la toile d'araignée

567   cobweb

une tasse de **cacao** bien chaud

568   cocoa

la noix de coco

569   coconut

la morue

570   cod

Les grains de **café** viennent du fruit d'un arbre.

571   coffee

le cercueil

572   coffin

le serpentin

573   coil

la pièce de monnaie

574   coin

J'ai **froid**.

575   I am **cold**.

le col

576   collar

La sœur de Julie **collectionne** les timbres.

577   to **collect**

Le collège est une école pour les grands.

578   college

Les voitures **entrent en collision** quand les conducteurs dorment au volant.

579   to **collide**

la collision

580   collision

Quelle est ta **couleur** préférée?

581   color/colours*

Le poulain est le petit de la jument.

582   colt

deux **colonnes** de pierre

583   column

le peigne

584   comb

Sandra **se peigne** les cheveux.

585   to **comb**

mélanger les ingrédients

586   combine

venir

Julie **est venue** à la fête en autobus.
Vous **venez** souvent ici?
Dis-lui de **venir** à la maison!

*Julie came to the party by bus.
Do you come here often?
Tell him to come home!*

587   to **come**

La poignée **s'est détachée**.

588   to **come off**

Il **revient à lui**.

589   to **come to**

confortable

590   comfortable

la virgule

591   comma

commander

592   to **command**

la communauté

C'est grâce à un effort de la **communauté** que l'école a été construite.
Il y a une piscine au centre **communautaire**.

*Building the school was a community effort.
There is a pool at the community center.*

593   community

deux **compagnons** inséparables

594   companion

Je suis en bonne **compagnie**.

595   I am in good **company**.

comparer

596   to **compare**

Ma **boussole** indique le nord.

597   My **compass** points north.

Jean-Sébastien **compose** une symphonie.

598 to compose

le compositeur

599 composer

une composition au piano

600 composition

un ordinateur

601 computer

Monique se **concentre** sur son travail.

602 to concentrate

le concert

603 concert

le béton

604 concrete

le chef d'orchestre

605 conductor

le cône

607 cone

le cornet de crème glacée

608 ice cream cone

la pomme de pin

609 pine cone

le chef de train

606 conductor/guard*

L'acrobate est **sûr** de lui.

610 confident

Je suis **un peu perdu**.

611 I am confused

féliciter le gagnant

612 to congratulate

connecter

613 to connect

une consonne

B, c, d, f, g sont des **consonnes**.

B, c, d, f, g are consonants.

614 consonant

une agente de police

615 constable

Une constellation a beaucoup d'étoiles.

616 constellation

Il y a sept **continents**.

617 continent

la conversation	Papa est bon **cuisinier**.	Il **prépare** le petit déjeuner.	Ne mange pas trop de **biscuits**!
618 conversation	619 Dad is a good **cook**.	620 He **cooks** breakfast.	621 cookie/biscuit*
J'ai la main gauche dans l'eau **fraîche**.	des tuyaux en **cuivre**	**copier**	un banc de **corail**
622 My hand is in the **cool** water.	623 copper	624 to copy	625 coral
le cordon, la corde	**le bouchon**	**le tire-bouchon**	Julie aime beaucoup **le maïs**.
626 cord	627 cork	628 corkscrew	629 corn/maize*
le coin	**le cadavre**	**le corridor**	**le cosmonaute**
630 corner	631 corpse	632 corridor	633 cosmonaut/astronaut*
L'actrice porte **un costume**.	**le chalet**	une chemise de **coton** derrière un cotonnier	**le divan, le sofa**
634 costume	635 cottage	636 cotton	637 couch/sofa*

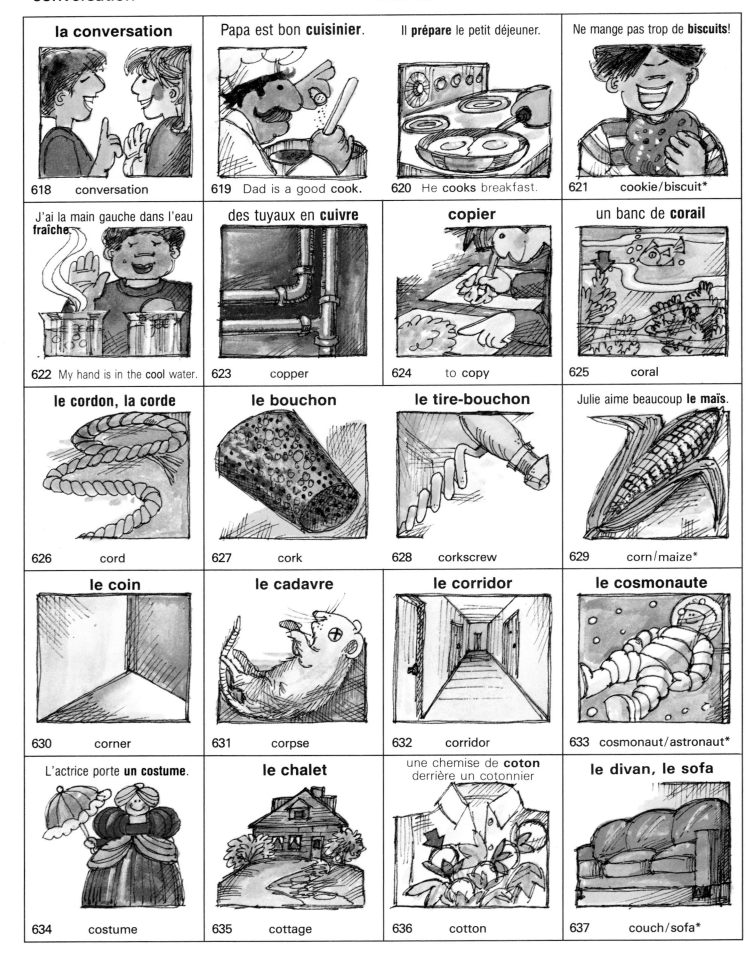

Amandine **tousse** poliment.

638　to cough

compter

639　to count

le compteur

640　counter

Mets-le sur **le comptoir**!

641　counter

Est-ce que tu vas souvent à **la campagne**?

642　country

Ce **pays**, c'est le Canada.

643　country

Maman et papa forment **un couple**.

644　couple

Il faut du **courage** pour se battre avec les dragons!

645　courage

le court de tennis

646　court

Ma **cousine** est la fille de mon oncle.

647　My **cousin** is my uncle's daughter.

couvrir

648　to cover

le couvercle

649　cover

la vache

650　cow

Ce garçon est **un poltron**.

651　This boy is a **coward**.

le cow-boy

652　cowboy

le crabe

653　crab

Le vase a **une fissure**.

654　crack

manger **un craquelin**

655　cracker

le berceau

656　cradle

la grue

657　crane

la grue

658   crane

heurter, tomber avec fracas

659   to crash

Qu'est-ce qu'il y a dans **la caisse**?

660   crate

ramper

661   to crawl

une écrevisse

662   crayfish

les crayons de couleur

663   crayons

la crème

Papa prend son café avec de **la crème**.
La crème glacée est très sucrée.

Dad likes cream in his coffee.
Ice cream is very sweet.

664   cream

le pli

665   crease

Quelle étrange **créature**!

666   creature

le ruisseau

667   creek

l'équipage du navire

668   the crew

le lit d'enfant

669   crib/cot*

le criquet

670   cricket

le criminel

671   criminal

le crocodile

672   crocodile

Les crocus annoncent le printemps!

673   crocus

L'escroc a volé une pomme.

674   crook

Le poteau est **tordu.**

675   crooked post

Le tableau est **penché**, la tour est droite.

676 crooked painting, upright tower

La récolte est belle!

677   crop

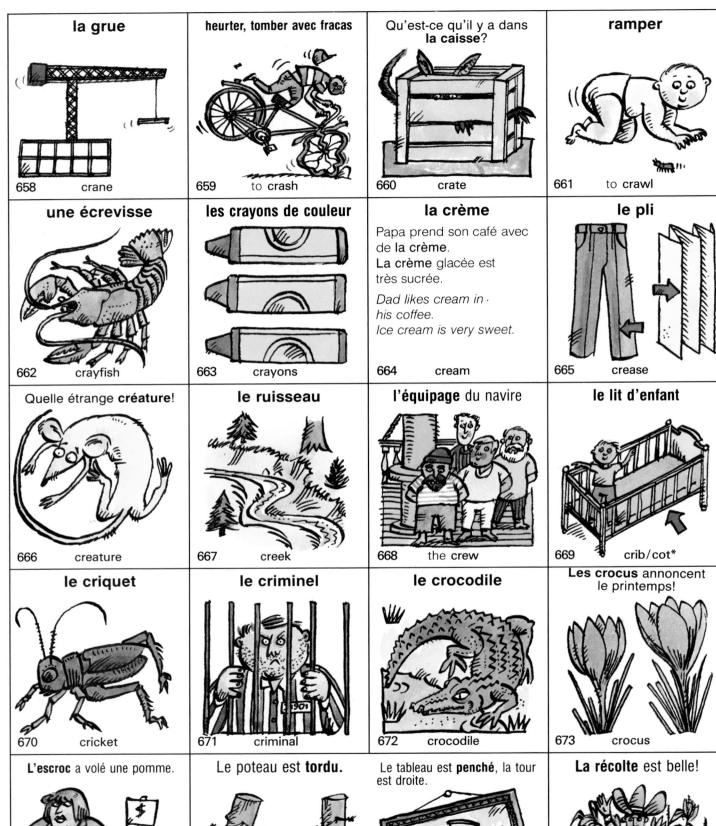

la croix

678   cross

Regarde avant de **traverser** la rue!

679   to cross

Le 6 a été **barré**.

680   to cross out

le corbeau, la corneille

681   crow

une foule immense dans un petit espace

682   A big crowd in a small space.

la couronne

683   crown

Le roi **couronne** la nouvelle reine.

684   to crown

les miettes

685   crumb

On **écrase** les raisins pour faire du vin.

686   to crush

C'est **la croûte** que Julie préfère!

687   crust

la béquille

688   crutch

pleurer

689   to cry

une boule de **cristal**

690   crystal

un ourson

691   cub

le cube

692   cube

le coucou

693   cuckoo

le concombre

694   cucumber

le poignet de chemise

695   cuff

la tasse de thé

696   cup

La confiture est dans **le buffet**.

697   cupboard

le bord du trottoir

698   curb/kerb*

Je suis **guéri**.

699   I am cured.

boucler, friser

700   to curl

les cheveux **bouclés**, **frisés**

701   curly

Hélène est **curieuse**.

702   curious

la groseille

703   currant

Le courant est fort.

704   current

les rideaux

705   curtains

la courbe

706   curve

le coussin

707   cushion

le client

708   customer

trancher, couper

709   to cut

Sandra est **mignonne**.

712   cute/sweet*

les couverts

713   cutlery

le cycle

714   cycle

couper la route

710   to cut in

le cylindre

715   cylinder

les cymbales

716   cymbals

le cyprès

717   cypress

Découpe la poupée en papier!

711   to cut out

Les jonquilles fleurissent au printemps.

718   daffodil

le poignard

719   dagger

Milou apporte **le quotidien**.

720   daily

la laiterie

721   dairy

Effeuillons ensemble **la marguerite**.

722   daisy

le barrage sur la rivière

723   dam

endommagé, abîmé

724   damaged

mouillé, humide

725   damp

danser

726   to dance

la danseuse

727   dancer

Le pissenlit est une mauvaise herbe.

728   dandelion

Attention! **Danger**.

729   danger

Luc n'a pas peur dans **le noir**.

730   dark

le jeu de **fléchettes**

731   dart

le tableau de bord

732   dashboard

Quelle est **la date** aujourd'hui?

733   date

C'est ma **fille** Pénélope.

734   daughter

le début d'**une belle journée**

735   the start of a nice **day**

La souris est **morte**.

736   **dead** mouse

sourd

737   deaf

---

cher

Mon **cher** ami.
Chère maman, il fait très froid ici et j'ai oublié d'apporter mon manteau.

My dear friend.
Dear Mother, it is quite cold here and I forgot to bring my coat.

738   dear

Décembre est le dernier mois de l'année.

739   December

---

décider

Julie n'arrive pas à **décider** comment s'habiller.
Peut-être Maman va-t-elle devoir **décider** pour elle.

Julie cannot decide what to wear.
Mother may have to decide for her.

740   to decide

---

le pont d'un navire

741   deck

Le pirate **décore** son arbre de Noël.

742   to decorate

---

la décoration

743   decoration

Albert évite le côté **profond** de la piscine.

744   deep end

Les cerfs vivent dans les forêts.

745   deer

---

livrer

746   to deliver

---

bosseler, cabosser

747   to dent

---

la dentiste

748   dentist

---

le grand magasin

749   department store

---

le désert

750   desert

Qui a mis ce **bureau** dans le désert?

751   desk

---

le dessert

752   dessert

---

démolir, détruire

753   to destroy

---

le contre-torpilleur

754   destroyer

Le détective enquête.

755   detective

Le matin, les feuilles sont couvertes de **rosée**.

756   dew

la diagonale

757 diagonal

le diagramme

758 diagram

le diamant

759 diamond

Bébé a besoin de **couches**.

760 diaper/nappy*

Suzanne tient **un journal**.

761 diary

Elle vérifie un mot dans **le dictionnaire**.

762 dictionary

mourir

763 to die

différence

Tous les gens naissent égaux, en dépit **des différences** qui les séparent.

All people are born equal despite the differences among them.

764 difference

des gens **différents**

765 different people

creuser

766 to dig

Le serpent **digère** un éléphant.

767 The snake **digests** an elephant.

La pièce est **sombre**.

768 dim

Julie a **des fossettes**.

769 dimple

le canot, le youyou

770 dinghy

la salle à manger

771 dining room

le dîner à la chandelle

772 dinner

le dinosaure

773 dinosaur

la direction à suivre

774 direction

Papa a marché dans de **la saleté**.

775 dirt

Ses pantalons sont **sales**.

776 dirty

Ils sont en désaccord.

777   to **disagree**

La pomme est disparue.

778   to **disappear**

Cet incendie est
un véritable **désastre.**

779   **disaster**

Le navigateur **découvre**
une île.

780   to **discover**

discuter

781   to **discuss**

la maladie

782   **disease**

Julie porte **un déguisement.**

783   **disguise**

Julie, où es-tu? Viens vite
faire **la vaisselle.**

784   **dishes**

une personne **malhonnête**

785   a **dishonest** person

l'eau de vaisselle

786   **dishwater**

Anna **déteste** les légumes.

787   to **dislike**

Le comprimé va se
dissoudre dans l'eau.

788   to **dissolve**

la distance entre
les deux arbres

789   **distance** between two trees

un arbre **lointain**

790   a **distant** tree

le district où j'habite

791   **district**

creuser **un fossé**

792   **ditch**

plonger

793   to **dive**

diviser

794   to **divide**

J'ai des **vertiges.**

795   I feel **dizzy.**

Que dois-je **faire?**

796   What shall I **do?**

le bassin	**le médecin**	**le chien**	**la poupée**
797 dock	798 doctor	799 dog	800 doll
le dauphin	**le dôme**	Cet **âne** porte un lourd fardeau.	**la porte**
801 dolphin	802 dome	803 donkey	804 door
la poignée de porte	**double**	**la pâte**	**La colombe** est le symbole de la paix.
805 doorknob	806 double	807 dough	808 dove
Julie a un oreiller en **duvet**.	**sommeiller**	**une douzaine** d'œufs	Ne **traîne** pas ton sac par terre!
809 down	810 to doze	811 dozen	812 to drag
le dragon	**la libellule**	**le drain**	Robert **dessine** bien.
813 dragon	814 dragonfly	815 drain/plug hole*	816 to draw

Relevez **le pont-levis**!

817   drawbridge

Les chaussettes de Julie ne sont pas dans **le tiroir**.

818   drawer

un beau **rêve**

819   a nice **dream**

Je **rêve** de moutons.

820   I **dream** of sheep.

la robe

821   **dress**

s'habiller

822   to **dress**

Les chaussettes de Julie sont peut-être dans **la commode**.

823   dresser/chest of drawers*

baver

824   to **dribble**

Quelle tristesse de **dériver** sans fin!

825   to **drift**

Patricia **perce** des trous.

826   to **drill**

la perceuse

827   **drill**

la boisson

828   **drink**

Le robinet **fuit**.

830   to **drip**

Je **conduis** prudemment.

831   I **drive** carefully.

Le conducteur a été imprudent.

832   crazy **driver**

Mistigris **boit** son lait.

829   to **drink**

la bruine

La **bruine** est une pluie très fine.

Drizzle is a very fine rain.

833   **drizzle**

Mistigris **bave** d'envie.

834   to **drool**

une goutte de sirop

835   **drop**

laisser tomber

836   to **drop**

Julien **est passé voir** Dominique.

837   to drop in

Papa **dépose** le chat chez le vétérinaire.

838   Dad **drops off** the cat at the vet.

abandonner la course

839   to drop out

J'**ai sommeil.**

840   I feel **drowsy.**

le tambour

841   drum

sec

842   dry

sécher

843   to dry

le nettoyeur à sec

844   dry cleaner

Mets le linge dans **la sécheuse!**

845   dryer

la duchesse

846   duchess

le canard

847   duck

le duel

848   duel

le duc

849   duke

le dépotoir

850   dump

déverser

851   to dump

le camion-benne

852   dumptruck/lorry*

Le prisonnier est enfermé dans **le donjon.**

853   dungeon

le crépuscule

854   dusk

Jeanne enlève **la poussière** avec son plumeau.

855   dust

le nain

856   dwarf

E

Chaque lapin a une carotte.

857   **Each** rabbit has a carrot.

Les aigles sont devenus rares; il faut les protéger.

858   eagle

une oreille

859   ear

le soleil **matinal**

860   early

gagner, mériter

Maman **gagne** un bon salaire.
Julie a bien **mérité** des vacances.

Mother earns a good wage.
Julie has earned a holiday.

861   to **earn**

la Terre

862   Earth

creuser **la terre**

863   earth

le tremblement de terre

864   earthquake

le chevalet du peintre

865   easel

L'est est opposé à l'ouest.

866   east

C'est **facile** de nager.

867   Swimming is **easy**.

manger

868   to eat

prendre son petit déjeuner

869   to eat breakfast

déjeuner

870   to eat lunch

dîner, souper

871   to eat dinner/supper*

un écho

872   echo

une éclipse solaire

873   eclipse

L'arbre est **au bord de** la falaise.

874   The tree is at the **edge**.

une anguille

875   eel

La poule a pondu **un œuf**.	**L'aubergine** est violette.	**huit** insectes	**le huitième** poisson
876 egg	877 eggplant/aubergine*	878 eight	879 eighth
Éric joue avec **un élastique**.	**le coude**	**une élection** On tient **des élections** pour choisir un gouvernement. Qui a remporté **l'élection**? *Elections are held to choose the government. Who won the election?*	**un électricien**
880 elastic	881 elbow	882 election	883 electrician
l'électricité	**un éléphant**	Béatrice attend **l'ascenseur**.	**un élan**
884 electricity	885 elephant	886 elevator/lift*	887 elk
un orme	**embarrasser, déconcerter**	**serrer dans ses bras**	**la broderie**
888 elm	889 to embarrass	890 to embrace	891 embroidery
une urgence	La boîte est **vide**.	C'est **la fin** de la route.	Un jour ils ne seront peut-être plus **ennemis**.
892 emergency	893 The jar is **empty**.	894 This is the **end**.	895 enemies

le moteur de l'auto

896   engine

le conducteur du train

897   engineer/engine driver*

savourer, apprécier

898   to enjoy

un dinosaure **énorme**

899   enormous dinosaur

C'est **assez**.

900   That is **enough**.

Milou **entre** par la porte.

901   to enter

une entrée

902   entrance

une enveloppe

903   envelope

des boucs de force **égale**

904   equal

L'équateur divise la Terre en deux hémisphères.

905   equator

la commission, la course

Julie fait **une commission** pour Papa.
Elle a beaucoup de **courses** à faire ce matin.

Julie is running an errand for Dad.
She has many errands this morning.

906   errand

un escalier roulant

907   escalator

La souris **s'enfuit**.

908   to escape

L'Europe est un continent.

909   Europe

Une évaporation se produit à cause de la chaleur du soleil.

910   evaporation

Quatre est un chiffre **pair**.

911   Four is an **even** number.

une surface **lisse**

912   an **even** surface

Le sapin est **un arbre à feuilles persistantes**.

913   evergreen

chaque

Julie fait son lit presque **chaque** matin.
Est-ce que Maman doit lui rappeler de le faire **chaque** matin?

Julie makes her bed almost every morning.
Must Mother tell her every morning?

914   every

un examen facile

915   exam

examiner à la loupe

916   to examine

un exemple

Parfois, Julie ne montre pas **le bon exemple**.
Il est plus facile de comprendre avec **un exemple**.

Sometimes, Julie does not set a good example.
Things are easier to understand when you give an example.

917   example

le point d'exclamation

918   exclamation mark

Pardonnez-moi, excusez-moi!

919   Excuse me!

Corinne fait des exercices.

920   to exercise

exister

Exister, c'est être.
Les dinosaures n'**existent** plus.

To exist is to be.
Dinosaurs no longer exist.

921   to exist

sortir

922   to exit/leave*

gonfler un ballon

923   to expand

attendre, s'attendre à

Nous vous **attendons** à deux heures.
Papa **s'attend à** ce que tu sois sage.

We expect you at two o'clock.
Dad expects you to be good.

924   to expect

Une montre **chère** coûte beaucoup d'argent

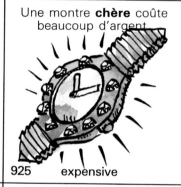

925   expensive

faire une expérience

926   experiment

une experte

927   expert

Serge **explique** à Milou qu'il doit obéir.

928   to explain

L'aventurier **explore** la jungle.

929   to explore

une explosion

930   explosion

un extincteur

931   extinguisher

un œil

932   eye

le sourcil

933   eyebrow

les lunettes

934   eyeglasses/spectacles*

les cils

935   eyelash

la fable de la cigale et de la fourmi

936   fable

le visage, la face

937   face

une usine

938   factory

Thomas **a échoué** à son examen.

939   to fail

tomber en panne

940   to fail

la foire

941   fair

La fée exaucera ton vœu.

942   fairy

la foi, la confiance

Nous avons **confiance** en toi.
Julie l'a accepté de bonne **foi**.

*We have faith in you.
Julie accepted it in good faith.*

943   faith

le **faux** tableau

944   fake painting

En **automne**, les feuilles tombent.

945   fall/autumn*

tomber

946   to fall

C'était une **fausse** alerte!

949   false alarm

la famille

950   family

tomber par terre

947   to fall down

faire une chute

948   to fall off

Brigitte est une **célèbre** actrice.

951   famous actress

le ventilateur

952   fan

une tenue **élégante, habillée**

953   fancy clothes

le croc

954   fang

La ville est loin.

955   The city is **far** away.

Adieu!

956   Farewell !

la ferme

957   farm

le fermier, l'agriculteur

958   farmer

rapide

959   fast

J'attache ma ceinture.

960   I **fasten** my seatbelt.

gros, gras

961   fat

Ce poison est mortel.

962   fatal

le père

963   father

Le robinet fuit.

964   faucet/tap*

À qui la faute?

965   Whose **fault** is it?

la faveur, le service

Puis-je vous demander **une faveur?**
Julie est gentille et elle aime rendre **service.**

Can I ask you a favor/favour?*
Julie is kind and likes doing people favors/favours.*

966   favor/favour*

ma saveur favorite

967   favorite/favourite*

craindre le pire

968   to **fear** the worst

le banquet

969   feast

la plume d'un oiseau

970   feather

Février est le deuxième mois de l'année.

971   February

nourrir, alimenter

972   to **feed**

Je me sens bien.

973   I **feel** well.

La femelle pond les œufs.

974   female

la clôture	**une aile d'auto**
975 fence	976 fender/wing*
la fougère	Paul et Anne prennent **le traversier**.
977 fern	978 ferry
le festival	Patrick a de **la fièvre**.
979 festival	980 fever
Peu de gens sont venus.	**le champ**
981 Few people came.	982 field
Alice est **la cinquième**.	**se battre, se bagarrer**
983 fifth	984 to fight
Régine se **lime** les ongles.	**remplir, emplir**
985 to file	986 to fill
Luce a **un film** pour son appareil-photo.	**sale, dégoûtant**
988 film	989 filthy
la nageoire d'un requin	**remplir, faire le plein**
990 fin	987 to fill up
L'agent lui donne **une amende**.	Je vais **bien**.
991 fine	992 I am fine.
le doigt	**une empreinte digitale**
993 finger	994 fingerprint

Joëlle **finit** première.

995   to finish

Le sapin a des aiguilles.

996   fir

le feu

997   fire

la voiture de pompiers

998   fire engine

la sortie de secours

999   fire escape

Les **pétards** peuvent être dangereux!

1000   firecracker/banger*

le pompier

1001   firefighter

un âtre, **la cheminée**, **le foyer**

1002   fireplace

ferme

Julie a une poignée de main **ferme**.
La décision de Papa est **ferme**. Thomas n'aura pas d'autre glace!

Julie has a firm handshake. Dad's decision is firm, Thomas cannot have another ice cream.

1003   firm

le premier de la file

1004   first

le poisson

1005   fish

Jean **pêche** dans la rivière.

1006   to fish

un hameçon

1007   fishhook

le poing

1008   fist

cinq

1009   five

Crois-tu qu'il va savoir **réparer** la voiture?

1010   to fix

le drapeau des pirates

1011   flag

Les flocons de neige tombent du ciel.

1012   flake

la flamme

1013   flame

Cuicui **bat** des ailes.

1014   to flap

le feu de signal	**le flash**	**la lampe de poche**	**le flacon**
1015　　flare	1016　　flash	1017　　flashlight/torch*	1018　　flask
plat	Maman **aplatit** la pâte avec un rouleau.	Quel **parfum** préfères-tu?	Zap a **une puce**.
1019　　flat	1020　　to flatten	1021　　flavor/flavour*	1022　　flea
Luc **s'enfuit** à belles jambes!	**la toison** du mouton	Il est bien **en chair**.	**flotter**
1023　　to flee	1024　　fleece	1025　　flesh	1026　　to float
un vol d'oiseaux	**une inondation**	**le sol**, **le plancher**	Le boulanger fait du pain avec de **la farine**.
1027　　flock	1028　　flood	1029　　floor	1030　　flour
Le sang **coule** dans le tube.	**la fleur**	Luc a attrapé **la grippe**.	**le duvet, la peluche**
1031　　to flow	1032　　flower	1033　　flu	1034　　fluff

La limonade est **un liquide**.

1035   fluid

la mouche

1036   fly

la braguette des pantalons

1037   fly

Les oiseaux et les avions **volent**.

1038   to fly

la mousse

1039   foam

Impossible de voir clairement avec ce **brouillard**!

1040   fog

Plier comme indiqué.

1041   to fold

L'oie **suit** Jeannot partout.

1042   to follow

la nourriture

1043   food

le pied

1044   foot

le ballon **de football**

1045   American football

une empreinte de pas dans la neige

1046   footprint

J'entends **des pas** derrière moi.

1047   footsteps

pour

Tous **pour** un et un **pour** tous.
Pour le meilleur ou **pour** le pire.

One for all and all for one
For better or for worse

1048   for

Il **force** la porte.

1049   to force

le front

1050   forehead

La forêt est pleine d'animaux.

1051   forest

oublier

Notre chien **oublie** son nom.
Papa **a oublié** d'acheter du lait.

Our dog forgets his name.
Dad forgot to buy milk.

1052   to forget

pardonner

Je te **pardonne** si tu promets d'être gentil.
Julie **a pardonné** à son chien d'avoir mangé la poupée.

I forgive you if you promise to be good.
Julie forgave her dog for eating the doll.

1053   to forgive

la fourchette

1054   fork

le chariot élévateur

1055   forklift

la forme

1056   form/tailor's dummy*

Les soldats sont dans **le fort**.

1057   fort

de l'avant, hardi

Va **de l'avant** jusqu'à ce que tu arrives à la porte. Julie pense qu'il est trop **hardi**.

Go forward until you reach the door.
Julie thinks he is too forward.

1058   forward

le fossile d'un poisson

1059   fossil

une odeur **infecte**

1060   foul odor/odour*

les fondations de la maison

1061   foundation

la fontaine

1062   fountain

Le renard est un animal rusé.

1063   fox

⅛ est **une fraction**.

1064   fraction

L'œuf est **fragile**.

1065   fragile

le cadre

1066   frame

Est-ce que tu as **des taches de rousseur**?

1067   freckle

L'oiseau est **libre**.

1068   free

geler, congeler

1069   to freeze

Une pomme encore toute **fraîche** de l'arbre.

1070   fresh

vendredi

Une fois **le vendredi** fini, plus d'école jusqu'au lundi!

Friday means no more school until Monday!

1071   Friday

le réfrigérateur

1072   fridge

des amis

1073   friends

Charlotte l'**a effrayé**.

1074   to frighten

la grenouille

1075 frog

Je viens **de** la planète Mars.

1076 I am **from** Mars.

l'avant

1077 front

La vitre est couverte de **givre**.

1078 frost

froncer les sourcils

1079 to **frown**

Les fruits sont bien meilleurs que les bonbons.

1080 fruit

frire

1081 to **fry**

la poêle à frire

1082 frying pan

Les voitures ont besoin d'**essence**.

1083 Cars need **fuel**.

plein

1084 full

avoir du plaisir, s'amuser

1085 having **fun**

la caisse de charité

1086 charity **fund**

les funérailles

1087 funeral

un entonnoir

1088 funnel

drôle, amusant

Maman ne trouve pas ça **drôle**.
Une chose **amusante** s'est passée à l'école aujourd'hui.

Mother does not think that is funny.
A funny thing happened at school today.

1089 funny

Un manteau de **fourrure** en été!

1090 fur coat

la chaudière, le calorifère

1092 furnace/boiler*

le mobilier

1093 furniture

Plus de lumière! **Les fusibles** ont sauté.

1094 fuse

un chat **à longs poils**

1091 furry

un grand vent

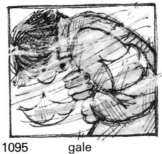

1095   gale

la galerie d'art

1096   gallery

Un cheval peut trotter ou **galoper**.

1097   to gallop

Noémie aime **les jeux**.

1098   game

Le jars est le mâle de l'oie.

1099   gander

une bande de voleurs

1100   gang

Julie a un **vide** entre les deux dents de devant.

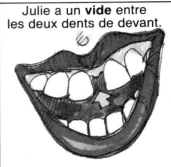

1101   gap

L'auto est dans **le garage**.

1102   garage

les ordures, les détritus

1103   garbage/rubbish*

la poubelle, la boîte à ordures

1104   garbage can/rubbish bin*

le potager

1105   vegetable **garden**

se gargariser

1106   to gargle

L'ail a un goût très fort.

1107   garlic

la jarretière

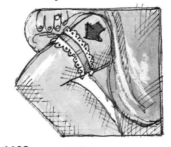

1108   garter

le gaz

Le ballon était rempli de **gaz**.
Certains **gaz** sont plus légers que l'air.

The balloon was filled with gas.
Some gases are lighter than air.

1109   gas

l'essence

1110   gas/petrol*

la pédale d'accélérateur

1111 gas pedal/accelerator*

la pompe à essence

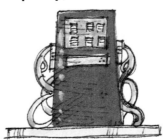

1112   gas/petrol pump*

la station-service

1113   gas/petrol station*

le portail

1114   gate

Louise **cueille** des fleurs.

1115   to gather

les engrenages

1116   gears

Le diamant est **une pierre précieuse**.

1117   gem

le général

1118   general

un ami **généreux**

1119   a generous friend

une personne **douce, gentille**

1120   a gentle person

Papa est **un** vrai **gentilhomme**.

1121   gentleman

un **vrai** cochon

1122   a genuine pig

Nous étudions tous **la géographie**.

1123   geography

le géranium

1124   geranium

la gerbille

1125   gerbil

Les germes provoquent des maladies.

1126   germ

Mistigris! **Attrape** cette souris!

1127   **Get** that mouse!

Je veux que tu me le rendes.

1128   I want to **get** it **back**.

Julie **entre** dans la piscine.

1129   to **get in** the pool

Julie **descend** de l'autobus.

1130   to **get off**

Elle **monte** dans le tramway.

1131   to **get on**

Elle **se débarrasse** des ordures.

1132   to **get rid of**

Mais d'abord, elle **se lève**.

1133   to **get up**

As-tu peur des fantômes?
1134 ghost

le géant
1135 giant

le cadeau de Rosalie
1136 gift

une baleine **gigantesque**
1137 gigantic

avoir un petit rire nerveux
1138 to giggle

les ouïes, les branchies
1139 gills

Le gingembre est une épice.
1140 ginger

un bonhomme en **pain d'épice**
1141 gingerbread

le gitan et sa roulotte
1142 gipsy

la girafe
1143 giraffe

Suzon est **une fille**.
1144 girl

Suzon **donne** un parapluie à Anne.
1145 to give

le glacier
1148 glacier

Je suis **content**.
1149 I am glad.

le verre
1150 glass

Anne **rend** le parapluie.
1146 to give back

Est-ce que tu portes **des lunettes**?
1152 glasses

glisser
1153 to glide

un verre d'eau
1151 glass

Je **me rends**!
1147 I give up!

Le planeur n'a pas de moteur.

1154   glider

des gants

1155   gloves

La colle tient bien!

1156   glue

aller, partir

1157   to **go**

le but

1161   goal

la chèvre

1162   goat

les lunettes protectrices

1163   goggles

Il **descend** travailler.

1158   to **go** down

le lingot d'**or**

1164   gold

le poisson rouge

1165   goldfish

Oncle Jean joue au **golf**.

1166   golf

Milou **entre** dans sa niche.

1159   to **go** in

Comme c'est **bon**!

1167   good

Au revoir Maman!

1168   Goodbye!

une oie

1169   goose

Jacques **grimpe** le long du haricot géant.

1160   to **go** up

les groseilles

1170   gooseberry

Elle pense avoir une coiffure **ravissante**.

1171   gorgeous

le gorille

1172   gorilla

gouverner

Le gouvernement **gouverne** le pays.
Ce n'est pas facile de **gouverner** un pays.

The government governs the country.
It is not easy to govern a country.

1173   to **govern**

le gouvernement

Le gouvernement est élu par les citoyens.
Le papa de Julie travaille pour le gouvernement.

The government is elected by the people.
Julie's Dad works for the government

1174   government

Luc **s'est emparé** de la glace de Lucie et il sera puni.

1175   to grab

Il est très **aimable**.

1176   He is very **gracious**.

Je suis en troisième **année**.

1177   grade / form*

Avec **le grain**, on fait de la farine.

1178   grain

1000 **grammes** = 1 kilogramme

1179   gram

---

le petit-fils

1180   grandchild

---

le grand-père

1181   grandfather

La grand-mère de Julie aime faire des gâteaux.

1182   grandmother

Le granit est une roche dure.

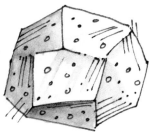

1183   granite

---

accorder

Je t'**accorde** dix jours de congé.
La fée t'**accordera** trois vœux.

I grant you ten days' leave of absence.
The good fairy will grant you three wishes.

1184   to grant

---

une **grappe** de **raisin**

1185   grapes

---

le pamplemousse

1186   grapefruit

---

le graphique, le diagramme

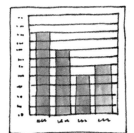

1187   graph

L'herbe est verte.

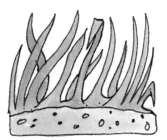

1188   grass

---

la sauterelle

1189   grasshopper

---

la râpe

1190   grater

---

la tombe

1191   grave

---

le gravier au bord de la route

1192   gravel

La gravité fait tomber les pommes.

1193   Gravity makes apples fall.

paître, brouter 1194 to graze	**La graisse** empêchera la porte de grincer. 1195 grease	un jouet **superbe** 1196 a great toy	**avide, cupide** 1197 greedy
vert 1198 green	**le haricot vert** 1199 green bean	**la serre** 1200 greenhouse	**saluer** 1201 to greet
La nuit, tous les chats sont **gris**. 1202 grey*/gray	**griller** 1203 to grill	**sale, barbouillé** 1204 grimy	Marc **a un grand sourire**. 1205 to grin
hacher, moudre 1206 to grind/to mince*	**saisir, agripper** 1207 to grip	**gémir, geindre** 1208 to groan	**L'épicier** renseigne la cliente. 1209 grocer
le marié et la mariée 1211 groom	**Le palefrenier** s'occupe des chevaux. 1212 groom	Patricia **se fait belle**. 1213 to groom	faire **des courses d'épicerie** 1210 shopping for **groceries**

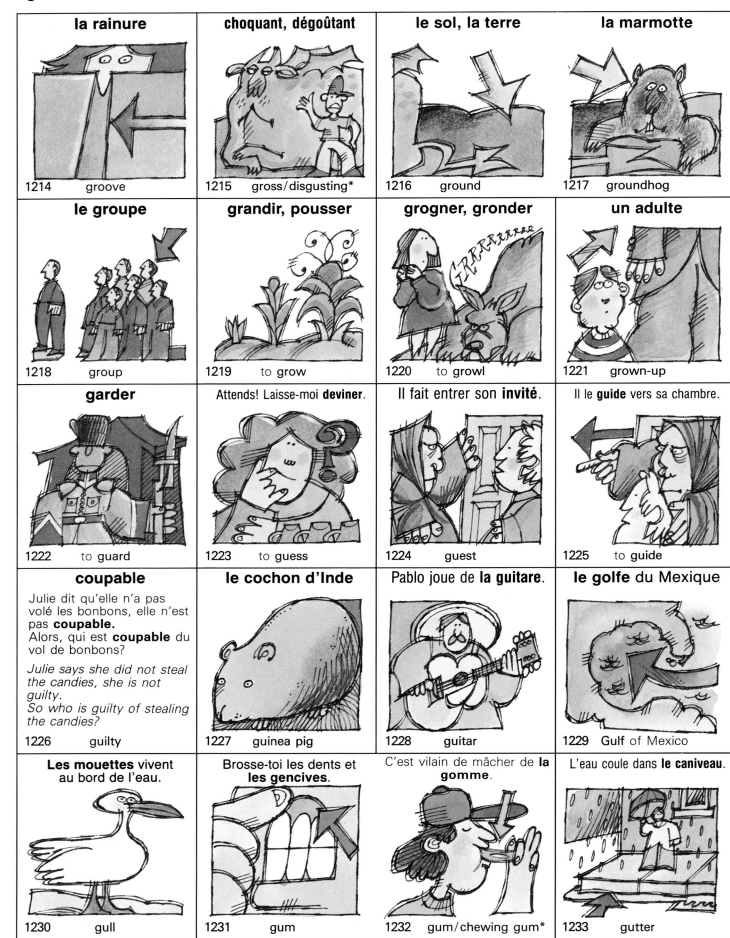

la rainure

1214 groove

choquant, dégoûtant

1215 gross/disgusting*

le sol, la terre

1216 ground

la marmotte

1217 groundhog

le groupe

1218 group

grandir, pousser

1219 to grow

grogner, gronder

1220 to growl

un adulte

1221 grown-up

garder

1222 to guard

Attends! Laisse-moi **deviner**.

1223 to guess

Il fait entrer son **invité**.

1224 guest

Il le **guide** vers sa chambre.

1225 to guide

coupable

Julie dit qu'elle n'a pas volé les bonbons, elle n'est pas **coupable**.
Alors, qui est **coupable** du vol de bonbons?

Julie says she did not steal the candies, she is not guilty.
So who is guilty of stealing the candies?

1226 guilty

le cochon d'Inde

1227 guinea pig

Pablo joue de **la guitare**.

1228 guitar

le golfe du Mexique

1229 Gulf of Mexico

Les mouettes vivent au bord de l'eau.

1230 gull

Brosse-toi les dents et **les gencives**.

1231 gum

C'est vilain de mâcher de **la gomme**.

1232 gum/chewing gum*

L'eau coule dans **le caniveau**.

1233 gutter

Fumer est **une** mauvaise **habitude**.

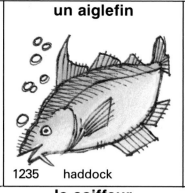

1234   bad **habit**

un aiglefin

1235   haddock

une tempête de **grêle**

1236   hail

La sœur de Julie a **les cheveux** drus.

1237   hair

la brosse à cheveux

1238   hairbrush

le coiffeur

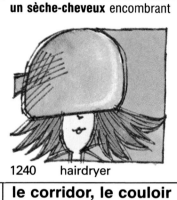

1239   hairdresser

un sèche-cheveux encombrant

1240   hairdryer

Veux-tu l'autre **moitié**?

1241   half

le vestibule, l'entrée

1242   hall

l'Halloween

1243   Halloween/Hallowe'en*

le corridor, le couloir

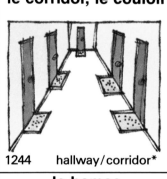

1244   hallway/corridor*

Le soldat **fait halte** devant la porte.

1245   to **halt**

le marteau

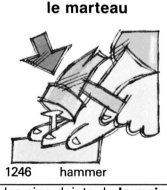

1246   hammer

Lucien **martèle** le morceau de bois.

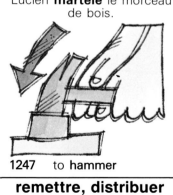

1247   to hammer

le hamac

1248   hammock

un hamster

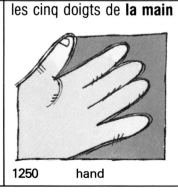

1249   hamster

les cinq doigts de **la main**

1250   hand

remettre, distribuer

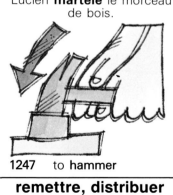

1251   to hand out

le frein à main

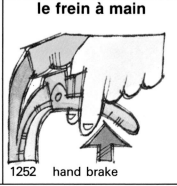

1252   hand brake

les menottes

1253   handcuffs

un handicap

Être aveugle, c'est **un handicap**.
Tout **handicap** peut être surmonté.

Being blind is a handicap.
People can overcome
any handicap.

1254   handicap

la poignée

1255   handle

la rampe de l'escalier

1256   handrail

Jerôme se trouve **beau**.

1257   handsome

Une personne **adroite** de ses mains.

1258   handy person

Suspends le tableau droit!

1259   to hang

Il **se cramponne**.

1260   to hang on

le hangar à avions

1262   hangar

Mets ta veste sur **un cintre**!

1263   hanger

le mouchoir

1264   handkerchief

Simon **accroche** le cintre.

1261   to hang up

Les accidents **arrivent**.

1265   Accidents happen.

Il est **heureux**.

1266   He is happy.

Les bateaux sont dans **le port**.

1267   harbor/harbour*

La pile de briques est trop **dure**.

1268   hard

le lièvre

1269   hare

Ce n'est pas bien de **faire du mal** aux animaux!

1270   to harm

un harmonica

1271   harmonica

La bride fait partie du **harnais** du cheval.

1272   harness

la harpe	un hiver **rigoureux**	Joseph **moissonne** le blé.	**le chapeau**
1273 harp	1274 a **harsh** winter	1275 to **harvest**	1276 hat
Ce poussin vient d'**éclore**.	**la hachette**	**tirer, transporter**	une maison **hantée**
1277 to **hatch**	1278 hatchet	1279 to **haul**	1280 **haunted** house
Marie **a** la poupée que veut Anna!	**le faucon**	**le foin** pour les chevaux	**La brume** rend l'air brumeux.
1281 to **have**	1282 hawk	1283 hay	1284 Haze makes for a hazy day.
le noisetier	**La noisette** est le fruit du noisetier.	**la tête**	J'ai **un mal de tête**.
1285 hazel	1286 hazelnut	1287 head	1288 I have a **headache**.
un appui-tête	Sa jambe **sera** bientôt **guérie**.	une fleur **saine**	**un tas** d'ordures
1289 headrest	1290 to **heal**	1291 healthy flower	1292 heap/pile*

J'entends une voix.	**Le cœur** bat dans la poitrine.	**chauffer, faire chauffer**	**le radiateur**
1293 I **hear** a voice.	1294 **heart**	1295 to **heat**	1296 **heater/radiator***
soulever	**le paradis**	un éléphant **lourd**	Pépé a taillé **la haie**.
1297 to **heave**	1298 **heaven**	1299 one **heavy** elephant	1300 **hedge**
Le hérisson a des piquants.	**le talon**	un **hélicoptère**	**L'enfer** n'est pas trop chaud pour ce diable.
1301 **hedgehog**	1302 **heel**	1303 **helicopter**	1304 **hell**
bonjour, salut	**la barre, le gouvernail**	Le soldat porte **un casque**.	Maman **aide** Papa à réparer l'auto.
1305 **hello**	1306 **helm**	1307 **helmet**	1308 to **help**
Un bébé est si **impuissant**!	**le bord, un ourlet**	La terre a deux **hémisphères**.	**la poule**
1309 **helpless**	1310 **hem**	1311 **hemisphere**	1312 **hen**

Un heptagone a sept côtés.

1313   heptagon

des herbes

1314   herbs

un troupeau de bétail

1315   herd

Viens **ici!**

1316   Come **here!**

Un ermite vit seul.

1317   hermit

le héros

1318   hero

une héroïne

1319   heroine

un hareng

1320   herring

Paul **hésite** à plonger.

1321   to hesitate

Un hexagone a six côtés.

1322   hexagon

Les ours **hibernent** en hiver.

1323   to hibernate

avoir le hoquet, hoqueter

1324   to hiccup/hiccough*

la peau, le cuir

1325   hide

Sidonie **se cache**.

1326   to hide

la cachette

1327   hiding-place

une **haute** montagne

1328   a high mountain

un grand immeuble

1329   highrise/tower block*

une école secondaire, un lycée

1330   high school/secondary school*

une grande route, une autoroute

1331   highway/motorway*

détourner un avion

1332   to hijack a plane

le sommet de **la colline**

1333   hill

la charnière

1334   hinge

les pattes **arrière**

1335   hind legs

la main sur la hanche

1336   hand on hip

un hippopotame

1337   hippopotamus

J'étudie **l'histoire**.

1338   I study history.

frapper, cogner

1339   to hit

Les abeilles vivent dans **la ruche**.

1340   hive

amasser, accumuler

1341   to hoard

la voix **enrouée, rauque**

1342   hoarse voice

un passe-temps, une marotte

1343   hobby

Mon frère joue au **hockey**.

1344   hockey/ice hockey*

la houe, la binette

1347   hoe

Julie **tient** Tigré sur ses genoux.

1348   to hold

Julie ne devrait pas le **maintenir à terre**!

1349   to hold down

la rondelle de hockey

1345   hockey puck

le trou

1350   hole

Oncle Jules a bien mérité **ses vacances** au bord de l'eau.

1351   holiday

Des écureuils vivent dans cet arbre **creux**.

1352   hollow tree

le bâton de hockey

1346   hockey stick

Le houx a des baies.	Il y a des pays où les vaches sont **sacrées**.	Les écureuils sont **à la maison**.	Luc fait ses **devoirs**.
1353 holly	1354 a holy cow	1355 home	1356 homework
Est-il **honnête**?	Les ours sont friands de **miel**.	**le rayon de miel**	**le melon vert**
1357 Is he **honest**?	1358 honey	1359 honeycomb	1360 honeydew melon
klaxonner	Quel **honneur** d'obtenir un diplôme!	Le manteau de Julie a **un capuchon**.	Le moteur est sous **le capot**.
1361 to honk	1362 honor/honour*	1363 hood	1364 hood/bonnet*
le sabot du cheval	**un hameçon**	sauter à travers **un cerceau**	**sauter, sautiller**
1365 hoof	1366 hook	1367 jump through a **hoop**	1368 to hop
J'**espère** gagner.	C'est **sans espoir**! Il ne saura jamais monter!	Aude joue à **la marelle**.	Le soleil se lève à l'**horizon**.
1369 I **hope** to win.	1370 hopeless	1371 hopscotch/hop-scotch*	1372 horizon

en position **horizontale**

1373 horizontal

un avertisseur, un klaxon

1374 horn

le cor d'harmonie

1375 French **horn**

la corne

1376 horn

Le frelon pique avec son dard.

1377 hornet

le cheval

1378 horse

Le raifort est piquant.

1379 horseradish

le fer à cheval

1380 horseshoe

le tuyau d'arrosage

1381 hose

un hôpital

1382 hospital

Il fait **chaud!**

1383 hot

C'est **piquant!** J'ai la bouche en feu!

1384 hot

En voyage, nous dormons à **l'hôtel**.

1386 hotel

Il y a soixante minutes dans **une heure**.

1387 hour

le sablier

1388 hourglass

le piment

1385 hot pepper

la maison

1389 house

un aéroglisseur

1390 hovercraft

Je vais te montrer **comment** faire.

1391 I will show you **how.**

Le chien **hurle** dans la nuit.

1392 to howl

un enjoliveur de roue

1393   hub cap

les airelles

1394   huckleberry

se serrer les uns contre les autres

1395   to huddle

L'éléphant est **énorme**.

1396   huge

la coque du navire

1397   hull

un oiseau-mouche

1398   hummingbird

Le chameau a deux **bosses**.

1399   hump

cent

1400   hundred

Elle **a faim**.

1401   She is **hungry**.

Joël **chasse** avec un fusil.

1402   to **hunt**

lancer

1403   to **hurl**

Qui donne un nom aux **ouragans**?

1404   hurricane

se dépêcher

1405   to hurry

Mon poignet me **fait mal**.

1406   My wrist **hurts**.

Édouard est **le mari** de Paule.

1407   husband

la hutte

1408   hut

le buffet

1409   hutch/sideboard*

la jacinthe

1410   hyacinth

La chorale chante **un hymne**.

1411   hymn

un trait d'union

«Après-midi» prend un trait d'union.

There is a hyphen in ''après-midi''.

1412   hyphen

La glace flotte dans le verre.

1413   ice

la glace, la crème glacée

1414   ice cream

Un iceberg peut faire couler un bateau.

1415   iceberg

De longs **glaçons** pendent du toit.

1416   icicle

le glaçage du gâteau

1417   icing

Elle vient d'avoir **une idée**!

1418   idea

des jumelles **identiques**

1419   identical twins

idiot

1420   idiot

oisif

1421   idle

si

Si j'avais un marteau,
je ne m'en servirais que
quand personne ne dort.

*If I had a hammer, I would
only hammer when no one
was sleeping.*

1422   if

un igloo

1423   igloo

la clé de contact

1424   ignition key

malade, souffrant

1425   ill

illuminer, éclairer

1426   to illuminate

une illustration

Dans un livre de contes,
il y a des mots et
des illustrations.

*Storybooks have words
and illustrations.*

1427   illustration

important

Ce qui est **important** pour Julie
n'est peut-être pas **important**
pour Luc.
Savoir lire et écrire,
c'est **important**.

*What is important to Julie may
not be important to Luc.
It is important to be able to read
and write.*

1428   important

en, dans

Nous faisons une
promenade **en** forêt.
Nous avons pris des
sandwichs **dans** notre sac.

*We are going for a walk in
the forest.
We have brought
sandwiches in our bag.*

1429   in

l'encens

1430   incense

Il y a douze **pouces**
dans un pied.

1431   inch

un index

Il y a **un index** à la fin de ce livre.
L'index contient tous les mots de ce dictionnaire.

There is an index at the back of this book.
The index contains all the words in the dictionary.

1432   index

L'indigo est un bleu violet.

1433   indigo

Marie a décidé de rester **à l'intérieur**.

1434   indoors

le bébé, le nourrisson

1435   infant

Tante Sylvie a **une infection**.

1436   infection

contagieux, communicatif

Sa maladie est **contagieuse**.
Papa a un rire **communicatif**.

Her condition is infectious.
Dad has an infectious laugh.

1437   infectious

Anne **fait savoir** à Paule qu'elle déménage.

1438   to inform

L'ours **habite** une caverne.

1439   The bear **inhabits** a cave.

Quelles sont tes **initiales**?

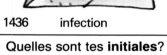

1440   initials

une injection, la piqûre

1441   injection

la blessure au doigt

1442   injury

L'encre est dans l'encrier.

1443   ink

un insecte

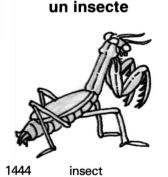

1444   insect

dedans, à l'intérieur

1445   inside

J'insiste pour que tu prennes ton bain!

1446   to insist

inspecter, examiner

1447   to inspect

Sers-toi d'une cuillère **au lieu** d'une fourchette!

1449   Use a spoon **instead** of a fork!

des instructions

1450   instruction

un instructeur

1451   instructor

un inspecteur

1448   inspector

une isolation

Il y a de **l'isolation** dans les murs de la maison.
Il y a de **l'isolation** autour des fils électriques pour que les gens ne s'électrocutent pas.

There is insulation in the walls of the house.
There is insulation around the wires so people will not get a shock.

1452   insulation

le carrefour, une intersection

1453   intersection/crossroads*

une entrevue

1454   interview

Daniel entre **dans** la pièce.

1455   into the room

Maman **présente** Jérôme à Jerémie.

1456   to introduce

Les Vikings **envahissent** le village.

1457   to invade

La guerre a fait **des invalides**!

1458   invalid

Qu'est-ce qu'il a **inventé** là?!

1459   to invent

un homme **invisible**

1460   invisible

Quel plaisir de recevoir **une invitation**!

1461   invitation

Il l'**invite**.

1462   He is **inviting** her.

un iris

1463   iris

Julien **repasse** ses vêtements.

1464   to iron

le fer à repasser

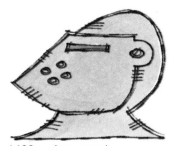

1465   iron

le masque de **fer**

1466   iron mask

une île

1467   island

la démangeaison

Marc a des **démangeaisons** causées par l'herbe à puce.
S'il arrête de se gratter, **la démangeaison** partira.

Marc got a bad itch from poison ivy.
The itch will go away if he stops scratching.

1468   itch

démanger

1469   to itch

La peau me **démange**.

1470   My skin is **itchy**.

Le lierre pousse sur les murs.

1471   ivy

	donner un coup	Est-ce que **la veste** est à sa taille?	**la jaquette** du livre
	1472 to jab	1473 jacket	1474 dust jacket

un bord **dentelé**	derrière les barreaux de **la prison**	**la confiture**	**coincer, bloquer**
1475 jagged edge	1476 jail/gaol*	1477 jam	1478 to jam

Janvier est le premier mois de l'année.	**le bocal, la jarre**	**la mâchoire** du requin	**le jeans**
1479 January	1480 jar	1481 jaw	1482 jeans

la jeep	**la gelée**	le moteur **à réaction**	un avion **à réaction**
1483 jeep	1484 jelly	1485 jet engine	1486 jet plane

le bijou, le joyau	**le casse-tête, le puzzle**	faire **un travail**	**le jet d'eau**
1488 jewel	1489 jigsaw puzzle	1490 doing a job	1487 jet of water

Le jockey monte un cheval de course.

1491   jockey

faire du jogging, courir

1492   to jog

joindre les deux bouts

1493   to join

le joint, l'articulation

1494   joint

Monsieur Croûton rit de sa mauvaise **blague**.

1495   joke

Le juge décidera.

1496   judge

le jongleur

1497   juggler

Annie aime **le jus** d'orange frais.

1498   juice

Juillet est le septième mois de l'année.

1499   July

La grenouille **saute**.

1500   to jump

Elle **saute dans** la mare.

1501   to jump in

Elle **saute sur** un rocher.

1502   to jump on

Gilles est **un** excellent **sauteur**.

1503   jumper

une barboteuse

1504   jumper/pinafore*

les câbles de démarrage

1505   jumper cables/jump leads*

Juin est le sixième mois de l'année.

1506   June

Il y a des tigres dans **la jungle**.

1507   jungle

La jonque est un voilier chinois.

1508   junk

les déchets, la camelote

1509   junk

juste

Juste un peu, merci.
Le juge est **juste**.

*Just a little, thanks.
The judge is a just person.*

1510   just

le kaléidoscope

1511   kaleidoscope

Le petit **kangourou** est dans la poche de sa mère.

1512   kangaroo

la quille du bateau

1513   keel

Milou aime sa **niche**.

1514   kennel

le grain, la graine

1515   kernel

la bouilloire

1516   kettle

la clé, la clef

1517   key

donner un coup de pied

1518   to kick

un enfant

1519   kid

Le chevreau est le petit de la chèvre.

1520   kid

enlever, kidnapper

1521   to kidnap

le rein

1522   kidney

Le chasseur **a tué** le lion.

1523   to kill

le four du potier

1524   kiln

1 **kilogramme** = 1000 grammes

1525   kilogram

1 **kilomètre** = 1000 mètres

1526   kilometer/kilometre*

En Écosse, les hommes portent **le kilt**.

1527   kilt

La robe est **une sorte** de vêtement.

1528   A dress is a kind of garment.

une **gentille** petite fille

1529   kind girl

Le roi porte une couronne.

1530   king

le martin-pêcheur

1531   kingfisher

le kiosque à journaux

1532   kiosk

le hareng doux

1533   kippers

embrasser

1534   to kiss

Fais-moi **un baiser**.

1535   kiss

la cuisine

1536   kitchen

Le cerf-volant fait des pirouettes dans le ciel.

1537   kite

le chaton

1538   kitten

Le kiwi est un fruit savoureux.

1539   kiwi

le genou

1540   knee

se mettre à genoux, s'agenouiller

1541   to kneel

le couteau

1542   knife

Est-ce que tu sais **tricoter**?

1543   to knit

le bouton de porte

1544   knob

Frappe à la porte avant d'entrer!

1545   to knock

le nœud

1546   knot

savoir, connaître

Sais-tu ce que cela veut dire?
Je ne vous **connais** pas!

*Do you know what this means?
I don't know you.*

1547   to know

une articulation

1548   knuckle

Les koalas vivent en Australie.

1549   koala bear

L

L'étiquette prévient du danger.

1550   label

le laboratoire

1551   laboratory

un col de **dentelle**

1552   lace

un escabeau, une échelle

1554   ladder

la louche à soupe

1555   ladle

la dame

1556   lady

Marc **lace** ses souliers.

1553   to lace

la coccinelle

1557   ladybug/ladybird*

les biscuits à la cuiller, les langues de chat

1558   ladyfingers

Le monstre est dans son **repaire**.

1559   lair

Le lac est au milieu des terres.

1560   lake

un agneau

1561   lamb

Le pauvre âne est **estropié**.

1562   lame

la lampe

1563   lamp

le réverbère

1564   lamp-post

la lance du chevalier

1565   lance

la terre

1566   land

L'avion **atterrit**.

1567   to land

le palier

1568   landing

le propriétaire

Monsieur Carpin paie le loyer à son **propriétaire**.
La maison appartient à son **propriétaire**.

Mr. Carpin pays rent to his landlord.
The house belongs to the landlord.

1569   landlord

Les autoroutes ont plusieurs **voies**.

1570   lane

la langue

Combien de **langues** parles-tu?
Le français est **la langue** maternelle de Julie.

How many languages do you speak?
French is Julie's first language.

1571   language

la lanterne

1572   lantern

Elle tient le bébé sur ses **genoux**.

1573   lap

le mélèze

1574   larch

Le lard fond dans la poêle.

1575   lard

grand

1576   large

une alouette

1577   lark

le cil

1578   lash

le **dernier** morceau de gâteau

1579   the **last** piece

Certaines choses **durent** vraiment.

1580   Some things do **last**.

fermer au loquet

1581   to **latch**

Tu es **en retard**!

1582   You are **late**.

la mousse de savon

1583   **lather**

rire

1584   to **laugh**

La chaloupe les emmène au rivage.

1585   **launch**

lancer une fusée

1586   to **launch**

la plate-forme de lancement

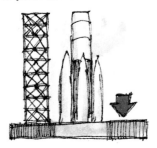

1587   **launchpad**

le linge sale

1588   laundry/washing*

Carole fait sa lessive à **la laverie**. **1589** laundry/launderette*	**La lavande** sent bon. **1590** lavender	Obéis à **la loi**! **1591** Obey the **law**!	Qui a tondu **la pelouse**? **1592** lawn
poser des carreaux **1594** to **lay** tiles	**des couches** superposées **1595** layer upon layer	Il est **paresseux**. **1596** He is **lazy**.	**la tondeuse à gazon** **1593** lawn mower
Vincent **mène** le cheval. **1597** to **lead**	**le chef, le guide** **1598** leader	**la feuille** **1599** leaf	Le seau **fuit**. **1600** to leak
La Tour de Pise **penche**. **1601** to **lean**	**J'apprends** à lire. **1602** I **learn** to read.	**la laisse** de Fido **1603** leash/lead*	Les chaussures sont en **cuir**. **1604** Shoes are made of **leather**.
Je **laisse** ce paquet ici. **1605** to **leave**	**partir, quitter** **1606** to **leave**	**le rebord** de la fenêtre **1607** ledge of a window	**le poireau** **1608** leek

Tourne à gauche!	**Il est gaucher.**	**la jambe**	**la légende** du cyclope
1609 left	1610 He is **left-handed.**	1611 leg	1612 legend
le citron	**la limonade**	Je te **prête** ce livre.	**la lentille, le verre de lunettes**
1613 lemon	1614 lemonade	1615 to **lend**	1616 lens
Le léopard est à l'affût.	**le collant**	Il y en a **moins** ici.	**la leçon**
1617 leopard	1618 leotard	1619 There is **less** here.	1620 lesson
Lâche-moi!	**la lettre** de l'alphabet	Julie a écrit **une lettre**.	**La laitue** pousse au jardin.
1621 **Let** me go!	1622 **letter** of the alphabet	1623 letter	1624 lettuce
le niveau	**le levier**	**Le menteur** a été puni.	Silence à **la bibliothèque**!
1625 **level** surface	1626 lever	1627 liar	1628 library

la plaque d'immatriculation

1629　licence plate/number plate*

lécher

1630　to lick

le couvercle du pot

1631　lid

Pinocchio est en train de **mentir**.

1632　to lie

La vie de ce bébé vient de commencer.

1634　life

le canot de sauvetage

1635　lifeboat

lever, soulever

1636　to lift

se coucher

1633　to lie down

la lumière de la lampe

1637　light/table lamp*

Papa **allume** la bougie.

1638　to light

une ampoule

1639　lightbulb

Elle **allège** la charge.

1640　She **lightens** the load.

le phare

1641　lighthouse

la foudre, un éclair

1642　lightning

le paratonnerre

1643　lightning rod

Cora **aime** bien son chat.

1644　to like

probablement, vraisemblable

Sophie ne viendra **probablement** pas demain. C'est une explication **vraisemblable**.

Sophie is not likely to come tomorrow. That is a likely explanation.

1645　likely

Le lilas fleurit au printemps.

1646　lilac

le lis

1647　lily

la branche de l'arbre

1648　limb

la lime, le citron vert

1649   lime

la limite

La limite de vitesse est de 30 milles à l'heure.
La bonté de Mamie n'a pas de **limite**.

The speed limit is 30 miles per hour.
There is no limit to·Mamie's kindness.

1650   limit

Notre voisin **boite**.

1651   to limp

la ligne

Peux-tu dessiner **une ligne** vraiment droite?

1652   line

Le linge est empilé dans l'armoire.

1653   linen

Le paquebot vogue sur l'océan.

1654   liner

la doublure de la jaquette

1655   lining

unir, lier

1656   to link

---

la charpie

1657   lint

le lion

1658   lion

les lèvres

1659   lips

le rouge à lèvres

1660   lipstick

L'eau et le lait sont **des liquides**.

1661   liquid

la liste

1662   list

Ils **écoutent**.

1663   They are **listening**.

le litre

1664   liter/litre*

Il ne faut pas **jeter ses déchets**!

1665   to litter

une **petite** pomme

1666   a little apple

vivre

Julie **vit** à la ville.
Il serait difficile de **vivre** sur la lune.

Julie lives in the city.
It would be difficult to live on the moon.

1667   to live

animé

1668   lively

le salon

1669   living room/lounge*

le lézard

1670   lizard

Le soldat **charge** le canon.

1671   to load

charger un camion

1672   to load

la miche de pain

1673   loaf

prêter

Sébastien **a prêté** de l'argent à Julie parce qu'elle avait dépensé tout son argent de poche.

Sébastien loaned/lent* Julie some money because she had spent her allowance.

1674   to loan/lend*

un **homard**

1675   lobster

fermer à clé, verrouiller

1676   to lock

la locomotive

1678   locomotive

le criquet, la sauterelle

1679   locust

le chalet de ski

1680   lodge/chalet*

la serrure de la porte

1677   lock

Le grenier est sous le toit.

1681   loft

la bûche de bois

1682   log

Laura lèche **la sucette**.

1683   lollipop

seul, solitaire

1684   lonely

La girafe a un cou très **long**.

1685   long

Lucien **regarde** par la fenêtre.

1686   to look

le métier à tisser

1687   loom

la boucle

1688   loop

Le bracelet est trop **lâche**.

1689   loose

Gérard **a perdu** une moufle.

1690   to **lose**

la lotion pour la peau

1691   lotion

La musique est trop **bruyante**.

1692   loud

le haut-parleur

1693   loudspeaker

s'étendre paresseusement

1694   to **lounge**

l'amour

L'amour est une chose très importante.
Julie pense que quand on a de l'amour, on a tout dans la vie.

Love is very important. Julie thinks that if you have love you have everything.

1695   love

Ils s'**aiment**.

1696   to **love**

belle, jolie

1697   lovely

la branche **basse**

1698   **low** branch

baisser, abaisser

1699   to **lower**

chanceux

Martin est **chanceux** de visiter la Suisse.
Julie est **chanceuse** d'avoir un si gentil petit frère.

Martin is lucky to be able to visit Switzerland. Julie is lucky to have such a cute little brother.

1700   lucky

les bagages

1701   luggage

L'eau **tiède** n'est ni chaude, ni froide.

1702   lukewarm water

Maman chante **une berceuse**.

1703   lullaby

le bois de construction

1704   lumber/timber*

Il a **une** grosse **bosse**.

1705   lump

le déjeuner

1706   lunch

la boîte à lunch, à déjeuner

1707   lunchbox

le poumon

1708   lung

le magazine, la revue

1709   magazine

Les asticots ne sont pas beaux.

1710   maggot

La magie est parfois étrange.

1711   magic

Un aimant attire les clous.

1713   magnet

un lion **magnifique**

1714   magnificent

La loupe grossit l'insecte.

1715   magnifying glass

Le magicien fait apparaître un lapin.

1712   magician

la pie

1716   magpie

poster, envoyer par la poste

1717   to mail/post*

Le facteur livre le courrier.

1718 mail carrier/postman*

Que **fait** Marc?

1719   to make

le maquillage de Mélodie

1720   makeup

le mâle et la femelle

1721   male

le maillet

1722   mallet

un homme

1723   man

La mandarine est un fruit juteux.

1724   mandarin

Il joue de **la mandoline**.

1725   mandolin

la crinière du cheval

1726   mane

La mangue est un fruit très sucré.

1727   mango

Il a de bonnes **manières.**
1728   He has good manners.

beaucoup
1729   many

la carte de géographie
1730   map

Le sculpteur taille **le marbre.**
1731   marble

marcher
1733   to march

Mars est le troisième mois de l'année.
1734   March

La jument est la femelle du cheval.
1735   mare

les billes
1732   marbles

le souci, un œillet d'Inde
1736   marigold

marquer la réponse correcte
1737   to mark

Tu as eu de bonnes **notes.**
1738   mark

le marché de fruits et légumes
1739   market

se marier
1740   to marry

le marais
1741   marsh

faire de la purée, écraser les pommes de terre
1742   to mash potatoes

le masque
1743   mask

Une masse a un poids.
1744   mass

le mât du voilier
1745   mast

Andrée **sait parfaitement faire** du vélo.
1746   to master

le match, la partie de tennis
1747   match

Il ne faut pas jouer avec **les allumettes**!

1748   match

les mathématiques

2
+2
4

1749   mathematics

une affaire

Tricher à l'école, c'est **une affaire** grave.
Le cerveau contient de **la matière** grise.

To cheat in school is a serious matter.
The brain contains grey matter.

1750   matter

Le matelas est vieux.

1751   mattress

Mai est le cinquième mois de l'année.

1752   May

peut-être

Julie devrait **peut-être** rester à la maison.
La réponse n'est ni oui, ni non : c'est **peut-être**.

Maybe Julie should stay home.
The answer is not yes, and it is not no, it is maybe.

1753   maybe

le maire de la ville

1754   mayor

Ne te perds pas dans **le labyrinthe**!

1755   maze

le pré, la prairie

1756   meadow

la grande sturnelle

1757   meadowlark

le repas

1758   meal

un **méchant** garçon

1759   mean person

Francine a **la rougeole**.

1760   measles

La règle sert à **mesurer** la longueur.

1 2 3 4 5 6

1761   to measure

la viande

1762   meat

le mécanicien

1763   mechanic

la médaille d'honneur

1764   medal

Le médecin prescrit **des médicaments**.

1765   medicine

moyen

1766   medium

rencontrer

1767   to meet

la réunion des professeurs	le melon	Le glaçon fond.	Notre club a quatre membres.
1768 meeting	1769 melon	1770 to melt	1771 Our club has four members.

le menu du restaurant	la merci, la pitié	la sirène	gai, joyeux
	Nous sommes à la merci du temps. Les bandits n'ont eu aucune pitié. *We are at the mercy of the weather.* *The bandits showed no mercy to anyone.*		
1772 menu	1773 mercy	1774 mermaid	1775 merry

un désordre terrible	Voilà un message pour toi.	la messagère	La chope est en métal.
1776 a real mess	1777 message	1778 messenger	1779 metal

Les météorites tombent du ciel.	le compteur	le mètre	la méthode
			Julie a une méthode pour apprendre vite. Une méthode, c'est une manière de faire les choses. *Julie has a method to learn quickly.* *A method is a way of doing things.*
1780 meteorite	1781 meter	1782 meter/metre*	1783 method

le métronome	le microphone, le micro	le microscope	le four à micro-ondes
1784 metronome	1785 microphone	1786 microscope	1787 microwave oven

midi	**au milieu**	**le nain**	**minuit**
1788 midday	1789 in the middle	1790 midget	1791 midnight

le mille	**le lait de la vache**	**Le moulin est au bord de la rivière.**	**l'esprit, l'intelligence**
Un mille a 5280 pieds. La vitesse limite est de 30 **milles** à l'heure. *One mile has 5280 feet. The speed limit is 30 miles per hour.*			$E = MC^2$
1792 mile	1793 milk	1794 mill	1795 mind

La mine est sous la terre.	**Ce mineur qui travaille dans la mine examine la roche.**	**les minéraux**	**le vairon, le méné**
1796 mine	1797 miner	1798 minerals	1799 minnow

Ces bonbons ont le goût de la menthe.	**moins**	**Il y a soixante minutes dans une heure.**	**un drôle de miracle**
	$7 - 5 = 2$		
1800 mint	1801 minus	1802 minute	1803 miracle

le mirage dans le désert	**le miroir**	**L'avare aime ses sous.**	**Ma famille me manque.**
1804 mirage	1805 mirror	1806 miser	1807 to miss

le missile

1808   missile

Michel s'est perdu dans **le brouillard**.

1809   mist

le gui

1810   mistletoe

le gant, la moufle

1811   mittens

mélanger

1812   to mix

le mélangeur, le mixeur

1813   mixer

le fossé, les douves

1814   moat

L'oiseau **se moque** du chat.

1815   to mock

un oiseau moqueur

1816   mockingbird

la maquette d'avion

1817   model airplane/aeroplane*

une chaise **moderne**

1818   modern chair

Sa couche est **humide**.

1819   moist

la taupe

1820   mole

le grain de beauté

1821   mole

Un moment s'il te plaît!

1822   One moment please.

lundi

Lundi est le premier jour de la semaine pour les écoliers.

Monday is the first day of the school week.

1823   Monday

l'argent

1824   money

le singe

1825   monkey

la lotte, l'ange de mer

1826   monkfish

Quel horrible **monstre**!

1827   monster

Il y a 12 **mois** dans l'année.

1828   month

le monument

1829   monument

Il est de bonne **humeur**.

1830   He is in a good **mood**.

Il est de mauvaise **humeur**.

1831   He is in a bad **mood**.

un croissant de **lune**

1832   moon

un orignal

1833   moose

le matin

1834   morning

le mortier et le pilon

1835   **mortar** and pestle

la mosaïque

1836   mosaic

Le moustique pique.

1837   mosquito

La mousse pousse sur les arbres.

1838   moss

la mère, la maman

1839   mother

le moteur

1840   motor

la motocyclette

1841   motorcycle

le moule à gâteaux

1842   mould*/mold

la motte, la butte

1843   mound

se mettre en selle, monter

1844   to mount

la montagne

1845   mountain

la souris

1846   mouse

Jules a **une** grosse **moustache**.

1847   moustache*/mustache

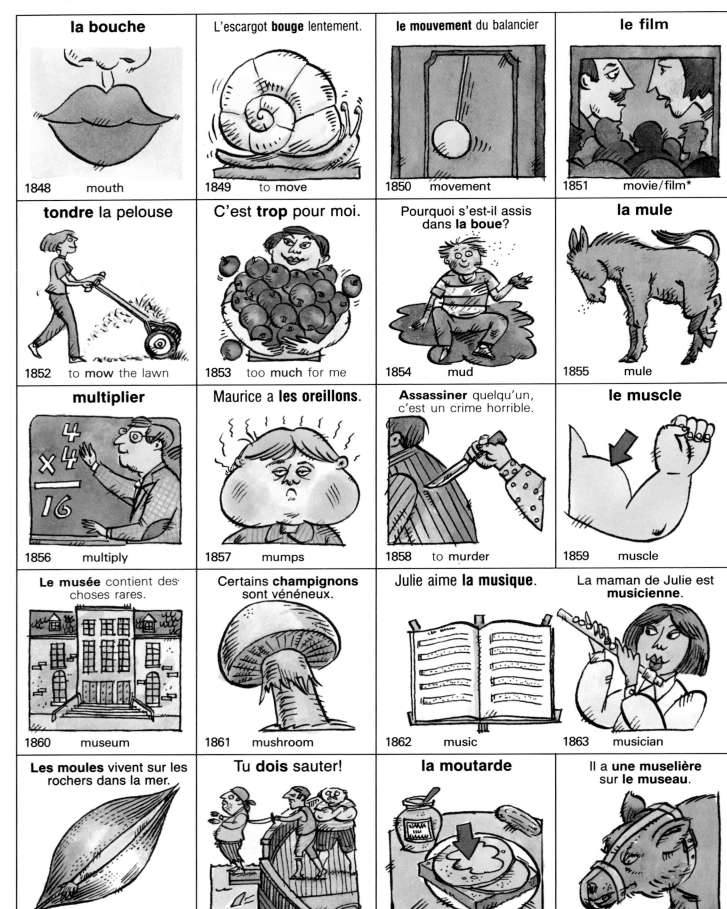

la bouche

1848   mouth

L'escargot **bouge** lentement.

1849   to move

le mouvement du balancier

1850   movement

le film

1851   movie/film*

tondre la pelouse

1852   to **mow** the lawn

C'est **trop** pour moi.

1853   too **much** for me

Pourquoi s'est-il assis dans **la boue?**

1854   mud

la mule

1855   mule

multiplier

1856   multiply

Maurice a **les oreillons**.

1857   mumps

Assassiner quelqu'un, c'est un crime horrible.

1858   to murder

le muscle

1859   muscle

Le musée contient des choses rares.

1860   museum

Certains **champignons** sont vénéneux.

1861   mushroom

Julie aime **la musique**.

1862   music

La maman de Julie est **musicienne**.

1863   musician

Les moules vivent sur les rochers dans la mer.

1864   mussel

Tu **dois** sauter!

1865   You **must** jump.

la moutarde

1866   mustard

Il a **une muselière** sur **le museau**.

1867   muzzle

N

le clou

1868   nail

un ongle

1869   fingernail

la pince à ongles, le coupe-ongles

1870   nail clipper

Ils sont tous les deux **nus**.

1872   naked

Mon **nom** est...

1873   My **name** is...

la serviette

1874   napkin/serviette*

clouer

1871   to **nail**

---

trop **étroit** pour passer

1875   too **narrow** to pass

Certaines **nations** sont des îles.

1876   nation

naturel

Les aliments **naturels** sont bons à la santé.
Les fruits contiennent du sucre **naturel**.

It is healthy to eat natural foods.
Fruit contains natural sugar.

1877   natural

La nature est belle.

1878   nature

Elle est **méchante.**

1879   She is **naughty.**

La capitaine **navigue** à l'étoile.

1880   to **navigate**

Elle est tout **près** du but.

1881   near

net, propre

1882   neat

---

pas agréable, mais **nécessaire**

1883 Not pleasant, but **necessary.**

le cou

1884   neck

le collier

1885   necklace

L'abeille fait du miel avec **le nectar**.

1886   nectar

la nectarine, le brugnon

1887   nectarine

le besoin

Julie aide toujours ses amis quand ils sont dans **le besoin**.
Se loger et manger sont **des besoins** fondamentaux.

Julie always helps her friends in need.
Food and shelter are basic human needs.

1888   need

J'ai besoin d'eau.

1889   I **need** water.

Tu sais enfiler une aiguille?

1890   needle

Il néglige son chien.

1891   He **neglects** his dog.

Le cheval hennit.

1892   to neigh

les voisins

1893   neighbors/neighbours*

Ni l'une ni l'autre ne me va.

1894   neither one fits

une enseigne au néon

1895   neon sign

Mon neveu est le fils de mon frère.

1896   My **nephew** is my brother's son.

le nerf

1897   nerve

Robert est nerveux.

1898   nervous

deux œufs dans le nid

1899   nest

Les orties piquent.

1900   nettle

Ne joue jamais avec le feu!

1901   Never play with fire!

un chapeau neuf

1902   new

les nouvelles

Maman lit les **nouvelles**.
J'ai de bonnes **nouvelles** pour toi!

Mother reads the news.
I have good news for you!

1903   news

le journal

1904   newspaper

Au suivant!

1905   Next !

grignoter, ronger

1906   to nibble

L'un des deux est **gentil**.

1907   nice

le nickel

1908   nickel

le surnom

Son prénom est Ariane, mais son **surnom** est Nanou.

Her name is Ariane, but her nickname is Nanou.

1909   nickname

Ma **nièce** est la fille de mon frère.

1910   My **nièce** is my brother's daughter.

Les hiboux chassent **la nuit**.

1911   night

le rossignol

1912   nightingale

Bastien fait **un cauchemar**.

1913   nightmare

neuf

1914   nine

La réponse est **non**.

1916   no

noble

Sir Du Val est **noble** et généreux. Aider une vieille dame à traverser la rue est une action **noble**.

Sir Du Val is noble and generous. Helping an old lady across the street is a noble deed.

1917   noble

le gentilhomme

1918   nobleman

le neuvième

1915   ninth

Il n'y a **personne** ici.

1919   nobody

le bruit

1920   noise

À **midi**, le soleil est au zénith.

1921   noon

le nord

1922   north

J'ai une mouche sur **le nez**!

1923   nose

la noix

1924   nuts

le casse-noix

1925   nutcracker

les bas de nylon

1926   nylon stockings/tights*

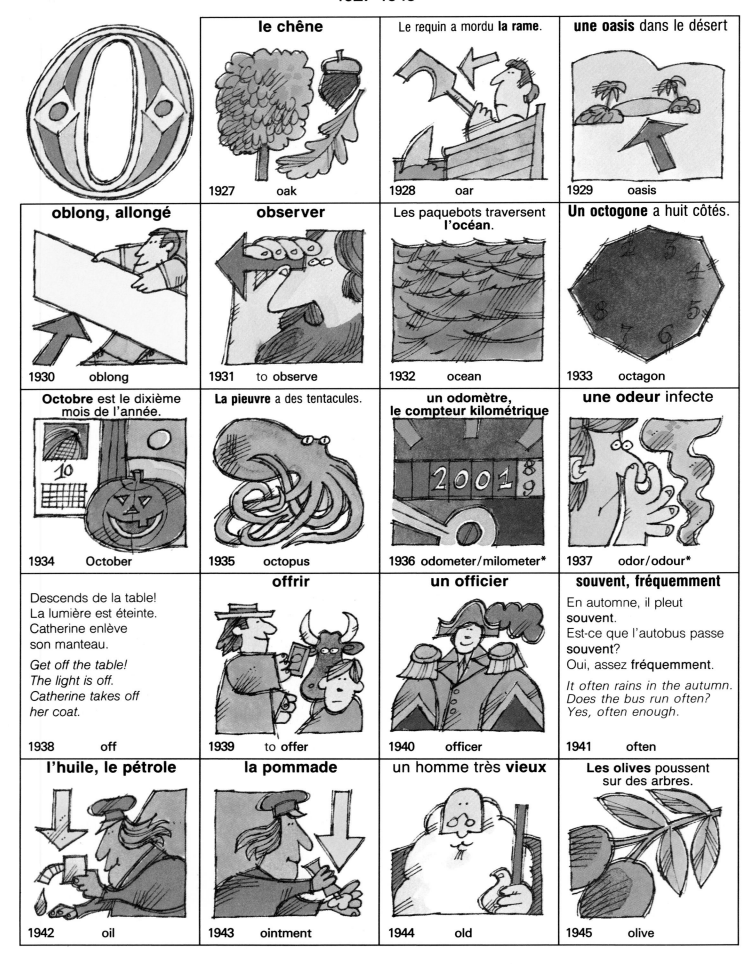

	le chêne	Le requin a mordu **la rame**.	**une oasis** dans le désert
	1927 oak	1928 oar	1929 oasis

oblong, allongé	**observer**	Les paquebots traversent **l'océan**.	**Un octogone** a huit côtés.
1930 oblong	1931 to observe	1932 ocean	1933 octagon

Octobre est le dixième mois de l'année.	**La pieuvre** a des tentacules.	**un odomètre,** **le compteur kilométrique**	**une odeur** infecte
1934 October	1935 octopus	1936 odometer/milometer*	1937 odor/odour*

Descends de la table! La lumière est éteinte. Catherine enlève son manteau. *Get off the table!* *The light is off.* *Catherine takes off* *her coat.*	**offrir**	**un officier**	**souvent, fréquemment**
			En automne, il pleut **souvent**. Est-ce que l'autobus passe **souvent**? Oui, assez **fréquemment**. *It often rains in the autumn.* *Does the bus run often?* *Yes, often enough.*
1938 off	1939 to offer	1940 officer	1941 often

l'huile, le pétrole	**la pommade**	un homme très **vieux**	**Les olives** poussent sur des arbres.
1942 oil	1943 ointment	1944 old	1945 olive

Le cuisinier fait une omelette.

1946   omelette

Le pot de fleurs est sur la table.

1947   on the table

une fois

Il était **une fois** une petite
fille appelée Julie…
Guillaume a voyagé en
Chine **une** seule **fois**.

*Once upon a time, there
was a little girl called Julie…
Guillaume has travelled only
once to China.*

1948   once

le chiffre un

1949   one

un oignon

1950   onion

mon seul amour

1951   my only love

Ne laisse pas la porte ouverte!

1952   open

ouvrir

1953   to open

**Jacques se sentira mieux
après l'opération.**

1954   operation

un opossum

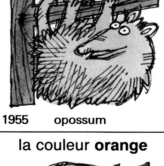

1955   opossum

contraire, en face

Le bien est **le contraire**
du mal.
La famille Gervais vit
en face de chez nous.

*Good is the opposite
of bad.
The Gervais family lives
opposite us.*

1956   opposite

ou

Tu peux faire tes devoirs
ou nettoyer ta chambre.
Préfères-tu une poire **ou**
une pomme?

*You can do your homework
or tidy up your room.
Do you prefer a pear or
an apple?*

1957   or

Il faut peler une orange.

1958   orange

la couleur orange

1959   orange

**Le verger est plein
d'arbres fruitiers.**

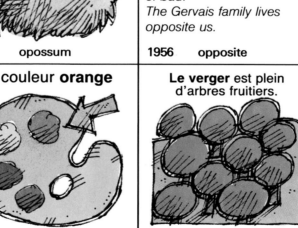

1960   orchard

un orchestre

1961   orchestra

une orchidée

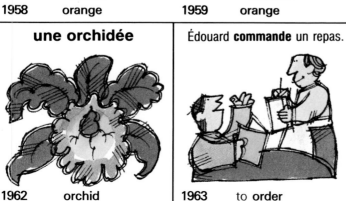

1962   orchid

Édouard commande un repas.

1963   to order

l'origan, la marjolaine

1964   oregano

Albert joue de l'orgue.

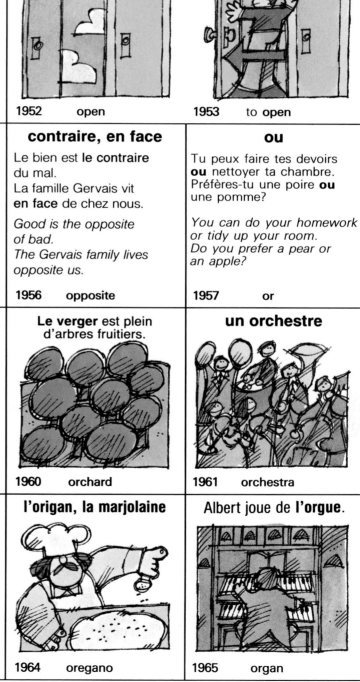

1965   organ

le loriot

1966   oriole

Un orphelin n'a pas de parents.

1967   orphan

Une autruche ne peut pas voler.

1968   ostrich

La loutre aime manger du poisson.

1969   otter

Il y a seize **onces** dans une livre.

1970   ounce

dehors, à l'extérieur

1971   outdoors

Tu aimes ma **tenue**?

1972   outfit

ovale

1973   oval

Il y a une tarte dans **le four.**

1974   oven

Un homme **à la mer!**

1975   Man overboard!

le pardessus

1976   overcoat

Le seau **déborde.**

1977   to overflow

la galoche

1978   overshoe

chavirer, se renverser

1979   to overturn

devoir

Mieux vaut ne pas **devoir** d'argent.
Tu **dois** le respect à ton professeur.

It is best not to owe any money.
You owe respect to your teacher.

1980   to owe

le hibou, la chouette

1981   owl

posséder, avoir

Nous possédons la maison où nous habitons.
Julie a 2 paires de chaussures.

We own the house we live in.
Julie owns 2 pairs of shoes.

1982   to own

le bœuf

1983   ox

Le plongeur a besoin d'**oxygène.**

1984   oxygen

Cette **huître** contient une perle.

1985   oyster

P

Julie **fait ses bagages**.
1986   to pack

le colis
1987   package

le bloc
1988   pad

Isabelle tient **la pagaie**.
1990   paddle

pagayer
1991   to paddle

le cadenas
1992   padlock

la plate-forme de lancement
1989   pad

Tourne **la page**!
1993   page

Le seau d'eau est lourd.
1994   pail

la peinture
1996   paint

Ne touche pas **la peinture** fraîche!
1997   wet paint

la douleur
1995   pain

le peintre
2000   painter

Bastien **peint** la barrière.
1998   to paint

le pinceau
1999   paintbrush

la peinture
2001   painting

une paire de chaussures
2002   a pair of shoes

le palais
2003   palace

Cette fleur est de couleur **pâle**.
2004   pale

la palette du peintre 2005 palette	**la paume** de la main 2006 palm	**la casserole** 2007 pan	Julie raffole **des crêpes**. 2008 pancake
le panda 2009 panda	**la console** 2010 panel	Fabrice joue de **la flûte de Pan**. 2011 panpipe	**la pensée** 2012 pansy
Blanchot **halète**. 2013 to pant	**la panthère** 2014 panther	**le pantalon** 2015 pants/trousers*	**La papaye** est un fruit comestible. 2016 papaya
le papier 2017 paper	**Le parachute** freine sa chute. 2018 parachute	**la parade**, **le défilé** 2019 parade	des lignes **parallèles** 2020 parallel lines
figé par la peur, **paralysé** par la peur 2021 paralyzed/paralysed*	Julie a reçu **un colis**. 2022 parcel	Le père et la mère sont **les parents**. 2023 parent	Grand-mère est dans **le parc**. 2024 park

garer, stationner

2025   to park

la parka

2026   parka

le parlement

2027   parliament

Le perroquet répète tout ce que je dis.

2028   parrot

le persil

2029   parsley

Le panais est un légume comestible.

2030   parsnip

Il y a **des particules** de poussière dans l'air.

2031   particle

le partenaire

2032   partner

la fête, la soirée

2033   party

Marie **passe** la balle…

2034   to pass

et Henri **tombe dans les pommes** sous le choc.

2035   to pass out

le passage

2036   passage

La passagère ne rame pas.

2037   passenger

Il faut **un passeport** pour aller à l'étranger.

2038   passport

passé

Dans **le passé**, il n'y avait ni avions ni autos.
Hier, c'est **le passé**; demain, c'est l'avenir.

In the past, there were no planes or cars. Yesterday is the past, tomorrow is the future.

2039   past

les pâtes, les nouilles

2040   pasta

Émile **colle** du papier peint.

2041   to paste

La broderie est **le passe-temps** favori de Marie.

2042   pastime

la pâtisserie

2043   pastry

le pré, le pâturage

2044   pasture

une pièce bien nécessaire

2045   patch

le chemin, le sentier

2046   path

Elle est **patiente**.

2047   She is **patient**.

Le patient semble inquiet.

2048   patient

le patron de couture

2049   pattern

**faire une pause,
s'arrêter un instant**

Après deux pages de
lecture, Julie **a fait une
pause**.
Il faut que je **m'arrête un
instant** pour reprendre
mon souffle.

*After reading two pages,
Julie paused.
I have to pause for breath.*

2050   to **pause**

marcher sur **la chaussée**

2051   pavement/road*

Combien de **pattes** a-t-il?

2052   paw

payer avec des pièces
et des billets

2053   to pay

le téléphone **payant**

2054 pay phone/phone box*

Paix sur la terre!

2055   peace

La pêche a un noyau.

2056   peach

Le paon fait la roue.

2057   peacock

le pic, le sommet

2058   peak

le son de la cloche

2059   peal of a bell

une arachide, la cacahouète

2060   peanut

la poire

2061   pear

La perle est logée dans l'huître.

2062   pearl

Les pois sont dans la cosse.

2063   peas

la tourbe pour les plantes

2064   peat moss

le caillou, le galet

2065   pebbles

la pacane

2066   pecan

picorer du bec

2067   to peck

la pédale du vélo

2068   pedal

Le piéton marche sur le trottoir.

2070   pedestrian

le passage pour piétons

2071   pedestrian crossing

peler, éplucher

2072   to peel

Mélanie **pédale** fort.

2069   to pedal

Le pélican a un bec très long.

2073   pelican

le stylo

2074   pen

le crayon

2075   pencil

Le pendule oscille.

2076   pendulum

le pingouin

2077   penguin

le canif

2078   penknife

Le pentagone a cinq côtés.

2079   pentagon

les gens, le peuple

2080   people

Les graines de **poivre** sont à côté du poivrier.

2081   pepper

la menthe poivrée

2082   peppermint

la perche

2083   perch

L'oiseau a trouvé **un perchoir**.

2084   perch

un spectacle très réussi
2085   performance

le parfum
2086   perfume

On met **un point** en fin de phrase.
2087   period/full stop*

La pervenche a des pétales bleus.
2088   periwinkle

la personne
2089   person

un insecte nuisible
2090   pest

Gaétan **embête** son papa.
2091   to pester

un animal familier
2092   pet

Combien de **pétales** a cette fleur?
2094   petal

le pétunia
2095   petunia

La pharmacienne vend des médicaments.
2096   pharmacist/chemist*

caresser, câliner
2093   to pet

la pharmacie
2097   pharmacy/chemist's*

le faisan
2098   pheasant

le téléphone
2099   phone

la photographie, la photo
2100   photograph

le piano de la maman de Julie
2101   piano

Choisis une carte!
2102   to pick

lever, soulever
2103   to pick up

la pioche
2104   pickaxe

les cornichons

2105   pickles

faire des conserves au vinaigre

2106   to pickle

un pique-nique à la campagne

2107   picnic

Le tableau de Pablo est très moderne.

2108   picture

la tarte aux cerises

2109   pie

Mmmm! **un morceau** de tarte!

2110   a piece/slice* of pie

Mélanie **joint** les deux morceaux de l'anse.

2111   to **piece** together

la jetée, la digue

2112   pier

le cochon, le porc

2113   pig

le pigeon

2114   pigeon

Le cochon est dans **la porcherie**.

2115   pigsty

le tas, le monceau

2116   pile

le comprimé, le cachet

2117   pill/tablet*

le pilier, la colonne

2118   pillar

Comme il fait bon dormir sur **un coussin** ou **un oreiller**!

2119   pillow

la taie d'oreiller

2120   pillowcase

le pilote de l'avion

2121   pilot

la verrue

2122   pimple

Le crabe a **des pinces**.

2123   pincers

Pincer fait mal.

2124   to pinch

le sapin

2125   pine

un ananas

2126   pineapple

la couleur rose

2127   pink

Maurice aime fumer **la pipe**.

2128   pipe

Le pirate est éclopé.

2129   pirate

la pistache

2130   pistachio

un pistolet ancien

2131   pistol

Georges **lance la balle**.

2132   to **pitch**

avoir pitié

Julie **a pitié** de Luc qui a perdu son chat.

Julie pities Luc, who lost his cat.

2136   to **pity**

un endroit, la place

Cet **endroit** est parfait pour un pique-nique.
Jean remet le marteau à sa **place**.

This place is perfect for a picnic.
Jean puts the hammer back in its place.

2137   place

le carrelet, la plie

2138   plaice

Bravo Georges, bien lancé!
Ce piano est mal accordé.

Hey Georges, that was a good pitch.
This piano is off pitch.

2133   pitch

Elle porte une chemise **unie**.

2139   **plain** shirt

La plaine s'étend sur des centaines de kilomètres.

2140   plain

L'architecte **fait des plans**.

2141   to **plan**

la fourche du fermier

2134   pitchfork

le rabot du menuisier

2142   plane

Les planètes tournent autour du soleil.

2143   planets

la planche

2144   plank

le goudron

2135   pitch tar

la plante   Le jardinier **plante** des fleurs.

2145   plants   2146   to plant

le plâtre   Elle **plâtre** le mur.

2147   plaster   2148   to plaster

Deux objets en **plastique**.

2149   plastic

la pâte à modeler

2150   plasticine

C'est **l'assiette** de Julie.

2151   plate

le plateau

2152   plateau

le quai de la gare

2153   platform

Ils **jouent** dans le bac à sable et dans **l'aire de jeux**.

2154   to play   2155   playground

les cartes à jouer

2156   playing cards

Il **supplie** le bourreau.

2157   to plead

une journée **agréable**

2158   a pleasant day

Un verre de lait, **s'il vous plaît**.

2159 A glass of milk, **please**.

le pli

2160   pleat

la pince, la tenaille

2161   pliers

Le fermier **laboure** son champ.

2162   plow/plough*

plumer une volaille

2163   to pluck

Branche le fil dans la prise!

2164   plug

Le fermier laboure son champ avec **la charrue**.

2165   plug

la prune

2166   plum

le plombier

2167   plumber

dodu, grassouillet

2168   plump

le pluriel

«Un» est singulier,
«deux ou plus» est **pluriel**.

''One is singular,
''two or more'' is plural.

2169   plural

Un **plus** un font...

2170   plus

le contreplaqué

2171   plywood

Jacques **fait pocher** des œufs.

2172   to poach

la poche

2173   pocket

la cosse du petit pois

2174   pea pod

le poème

Un poème est fait de vers qui riment.
Mais tous **les poèmes** ne sont pas sublimes.

*A poem has sets of lines which rhyme.
But not all poems are sublime.*

2175   poem

indiquer, montrer du doigt

2177   to point

la poinsettie

2176   poinsettia

le poison

2180   poison

vénéneux, vénimeux

Certains champignons sont **vénéneux**.
La plupart des serpents ne sont pas **vénimeux**.

*Some mushrooms are poisonous.
Most snakes are not poisonous.*

2181   poisonous

La pointe de la flèche est aiguë.

2178   point

pousser du doigt

2182   to poke

un ours **polaire**

2183   polar bear

le poteau

2184   pole

pointu

2179   pointed

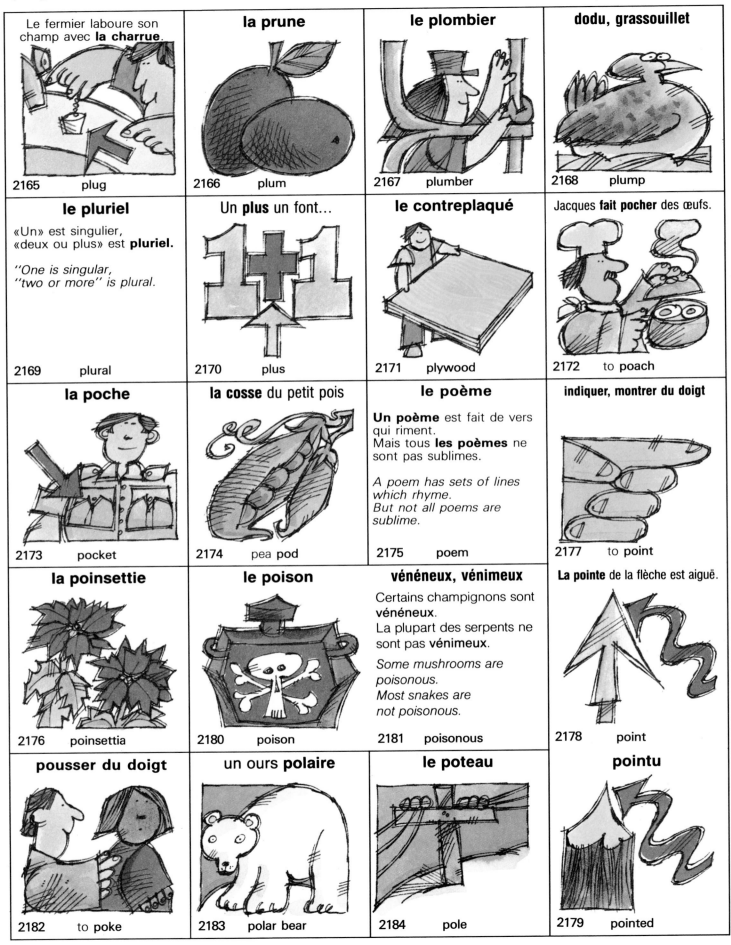

le policier, l'agent de police

2185   policeman

l'agente de police

2186   policewoman

polir, lisser

2187   to polish

poli

Ce n'est pas **poli** de crier.
Le professeur attend une réponse **polie**.

*It is not polite to shout.
The teacher expects a polite answer.*

2188   polite

Julie est allergique au **pollen** des fleurs.

2189   pollen

La grenade est un fruit.

2190   pomegranate

un étang au milieu des bois

2191   pond

le poney de Joséphine

2192   pony

Ils nagent dans **la piscine**.

2193   pool

mettre en commun

2194   to pool

pauvre, piètre

Sa famille n'est ni **pauvre**, ni riche.
Julie a obtenu de **piètres** résultats parce qu'elle n'a pas travaillé dur.

*Her family is not poor, but it is not rich either.
Julie had poor results because she did not work hard.*

2195   poor

faire sauter le bouchon

2196   to pop

---

le peuplier

2197   poplar

le pavot, le coquelicot

2198   poppy

Beaucoup de gens aiment Julie.
Ce livre plaît à beaucoup de gens.

*Julie is a popular girl.
This book is very popular.*

2199   popular

le porche

2200   porch

Les pores sont des petits trous de la peau.

2201   Pores are little holes in the skin.

le porridge, la bouillie

2202   porridge

le port

2203   port

portatif

Julie veut une radio **portative**, mais elle n'a pas fait assez d'économies.

Julie wants a portable radio but she has not saved up enough money.

2204   portable

le porteur	**le portrait** de tante Alice	**le poteau, le pilier**	Pierre **poste** une lettre.
2205 porter	2206 portrait	2207 post	2208 to post
la carte postale	**une affiche**	**le pot**	**le bureau de poste**
2210 postcard	2211 poster	2212 pot	2209 post office
la pomme de terre	**la poterie, la céramique**	**la bourse, le sac**	**sauter, bondir**
2213 potato	2214 pottery	2215 pouch	2216 to pounce
la livre Quatre bananes pèsent environ **une livre**. *Four bananas weigh about a pound.*	**frapper, taper**	**verser**	**bouder**
2217 pound	2218 to pound	2219 to pour	2220 to pout
la poudre	**pratiquer, s'exercer**	Le blé pousse dans **la prairie**.	**louer, glorifier**
2221 powder	2222 to practice/practise*	2223 prairie	2224 to praise

Le cheval piaffe. 2225 to prance	**prier** 2226 to pray	**Je préfère celle-là.** 2227 to prefer	**Elle est enceinte.** 2228 She is pregnant.
Je suis présent. 2229 I am present.	**le cadeau** d'anniversaire 2230 birthday present	**présenter, décerner** un prix 2231 to present	**les conserves** de fruits 2232 preserved fruit
presser, appuyer 2233 to press	une **jolie** fillette 2234 pretty	La chouette a attrapé **une proie**. 2235 prey	**Le prix** est marqué sur l'étiquette. 2236 price
piquer 2237 to prick	un animal **armé de piquants** 2238 prickly animal	une école **primaire** 2239 primary school	la **primevère** à grandes fleurs 2240 primrose
le prince 2241 prince	**la princesse** 2242 princess	**la directrice d'école** 2243 school principal/Head teacher*	**le principe** En **principe**, je suis d'accord avec toi. **Le** premier **principe**, c'est de travailler dur. *In principle, I agree with you.* *The first principle is to work hard.* 2244 principle

imprimer	**le prisme**	Le voleur est allé en **prison**.	**le prisonnier**
2245 to print	2246 prism	2247 prison	2248 prisoner

privé	**le prix, la récompense**	**le problème**	**les produits** maraîchers
Julie et moi avons une conversation **privée**. C'est une propriété **privée**. *Julie and I are having a private conversation. This is private property.*			
2249 private	2250 prize	2251 problem	2252 produce

Il y a peu de bons **programmes** à la télévision.	**Interdit** aux chiens!	**le projet**	Cette usine **fabrique** des voitures.
		Lucie est en train de travailler à **un projet** difficile. Julie n'a pas bien réussi son **projet**. *Lucie is working on a difficult project. Julie did not do well on her project.*	
2254 program/programme*	2255 prohibited	2256 project	2253 This factory **produces** cars.

Je promets.	**la dent** de la fourche	**Prononce** bien tes mots!	**la preuve** de sa culpabilité
2257 I promise.	2258 prong	2259 to pronounce	2260 proof of guilt

appuyer, soutenir	**une hélice**	**correctement** vêtu	**la propriété**
			Julie dit «C'est à moi» quand elle veut dire «C'est ma **propriété**». Sa famille a **une propriété** à la campagne. *Julie says "This is mine" when she means "This is my property". Her family owns property in the country.*
2261 to prop	2262 propeller	2263 properly dressed	2264 property

manifester, protester

2265   to protest

Je suis un chat **fier**.

2266   I am a **proud** cat.

Je peux le **prouver**!

2267   to **prove**

le proverbe

Voici **un proverbe** :
«Pierre qui roule n'amasse pas mousse.»

*Here is a proverb:
"A rolling stone gathers no moss."*

2268   proverb

fournir des chaises

2269   to **provide** chairs

Un pruneau est une prune séchée.

2270   prune

tailler, élaguer

2271   to prune

le téléphone **public**

2272   public telephone/**phone box***

le pouding

2273   pudding/afters*

la flaque d'eau

2274   puddle

lancer des bouffées

2275   to **puff**

le macareux

2276   puffin

tirer

2277   to **pull**

la poulie

2278   pulley

le pull-over, le chandail

2279   pullover/sweater*

Le médecin lui prend **le pouls**.

2280   pulse

la pompe

2281   pump

Elle **pompe** de toutes **ses forces**.

2282   to **pump**

le potiron, la citrouille

2283   pumpkin

donner un coup de poing

2284   to **punch**

Tu es ponctuel.

2285   You are punctual.

percer, crever

2286   to puncture

Elle punit sa fille.

2287   to punish

la punition

2288   punishment

la marionnette

2289   puppet

le jeune chien, le chiot

2290   puppy

une eau pure

2291   pure water

violet

2292   purple

Les chats ronronnent quand ils sont contents.

2293   to purr

le sac, la sacoche

2294   purse/handbag*

Fido poursuit Chamarré.

2295   to pursue

pousser

2296   to push

mettre, placer

2297   to put

Il range son pull dans le tiroir.

2298   to put away

Il remet à plus tard sa lecture.

2299   to put off

Le mastic fait tenir la vitre en place.

2300   putty

le puzzle

2301   puzzle

le pyjama

2302   pyjamas*/pajamas

la pyramide

2303   pyramid

Le python broie sa proie entre ses anneaux.

2304   python

la caille

2305   quail

une montre de **qualité**

2306   **quality** watch

la quantité

2307   quantity

se disputer, se quereller

2308   to quarrel

Est-ce **une carrière** de pierres ou de sable?

2309   quarry

le quart

$\frac{1}{4}$

2310   quarter

Le bateau est amarré au **quai**.

2311   quay

la reine

2312   queen

poser **une question**

2313   to ask a **question**

rapide comme l'éclair

2314   quick

Il s'enfonce dans **les sables mouvants**.

2315   quicksand

Elle est **calme, tranquille**.

2316   She is **quiet**.

Autrefois, on écrivait à **la plume**.

2317   quill

les piquants du porc-épic

2318   porcupine **quill**

la couverture piquée

2319   quilt/eiderdown*

Le coing est un fruit âpre.

2320   quince

un carquois plein de flèches

2321   quiver

trembler, frissonner

2322   to **quiver**

le contrôle, la colle

Hier, nous avons eu **un contrôle** d'histoire. Aujourd'hui, nous avons eu **une colle** en classe de géo.

Yesterday, we had a history quiz.
Today, we had a geography quiz.

2323   quiz

R

le lapin
2324   rabbit

le raton laveur
2325   raccoon

Le lièvre et la tortue **font la course.**
2326   to **race**

le porte-manteau
2327   rack/hat-stand*

le tapage, le vacarme
2328   racket

Le radiateur chauffe la pièce.
2329   radiator

la radio
2330   radio

le radis
2331   radish

le rayon du cercle
2332   radius

Le radeau descend au fil de l'eau.
2333   raft

Une attaque a lieu.
2334   a **raid** in progress

Tiens bien **la rampe!**
2335   handrail/banister*

la voie ferrée
2336   railroad track/railway track*

Il **pleut** des cordes!
2337   to **rain**

Après la pluie, vient **l'arc-en-ciel.**
2338   rainbow

un imperméable
2339   raincoat

lever, soulever
Tous ceux qui veulent du chocolat, **levez** la main!
Elle **a soulevé** une question intéressante.

Everyone who wants chocolate, raise your hand!
She has raised an interesting question.

2340   to **raise**

les raisins secs
2341   raisin

le rateau
2342   rake

frapper à la porte
2343   to rap/knock*

rapide
2344   rapid

rare
2345   rare

une éruption de boutons
2346   rash

Les framboises sont des baies.
2347   raspberry

le rat
2348   rat

le hochet de bébé
2349   rattle

le serpent à sonnettes
2350   rattlesnake

Le corbeau a le plumage noir.
2351   raven

Elle semble **affamée!**
2352   ravenous

le ravin
2353   ravine

un œuf **cru**
2354   a raw egg

le rayon de soleil
2355   ray of sunlight

Le rasoir est très coupant.
2356   razor

atteindre
2357   to reach

lire
2358   to read

À vos marques... **prêts...** partez!
2359   ready

Est-ce que c'est un **vrai** diamant?
2360   real

comprendre, s'apercevoir, se rendre compte
2361   to realize/realise*

Es-tu **vraiment** là?
2362   Are you **really** here?

le derrière

2363   rear

le rétroviseur

2364   rearview mirror

raisonner

2365   to reason

raisonnable

C'est un prix **raisonnable**.
Julie, sois **raisonnable**
s'il te plaît.

This is a reasonable price.
Julie, please be reasonable.

2366   reasonable

se rebeller, se révolter

Les gens **se rebellent**
contre les impôts excessifs.
Spartacus **s'est révolté**
contre Rome.

People do rebel against
taxes which are too high.
Spartacus rebelled against
Rome.

2367   to rebel

Je ne **me souviens** pas.

2368   I do not recall.

Patricia vient de **recevoir**
un cadeau.

2369   to receive

récemment éclos

2370   recently hatched

la recette

2371   recipe

Elle **récite** un poème.

2372   to recite

un disque, un enregistrement

2373   record

le tourne-disque

2374   record player

guérir, récupérer

Julie a les oreillons mais
elle **guérira**.
J'ai **récupéré** tous les livres
qui étaient dehors.

Julie has measles but she
will recover.
I recovered all the books
that were left outside.

2375   to recover

le rectangle

2376   rectangle

rouge

2377   red

le roseau

2378   reed

le **récif** de corail

2379   reef

Comme ça **sent mauvais**!

2380   to reek

Le fil est enroulé sur **le moulinet**.

2381   reel

un arbitre

2382   referee

le reflet

2383   reflection

Ne laisse pas **le réfrigérateur** ouvert!

2384   refrigerator

refuser

2385   to refuse

la région

2386   region

s'inscrire

2387   to register

regretter

2388   to regret

Les acteurs **répètent** une pièce.

2389   Actors **rehearse** a play.

le renne

2390   reindeer

les rênes du cheval

2391   reins

la parenté

2392   relatives

se reposer, se relaxer

2393   to relax

relâcher, libérer

2394   to release

Souviens-toi de te brosser les dents!

2395   **Remember** to brush your teeth.

une île **éloignée**

2396   **remote** island

Philippe **enlève** son chapeau.

2397   to remove

louer

Nous louons une maison.
Si tu n'as pas de voiture,
tu peux en **louer** une.

*We rent a house.
If you do not have a car,
you can rent one.*

2398   to **rent**

Blandine **répare** son vélo.

2399   to repair

Le perroquet **répète** tout.

2400   to repeat

Suzon **remplace** l'ampoule.

2401   to replace

Thierry pose une question et Solange **répond**.

2402   to **reply**

le reptile

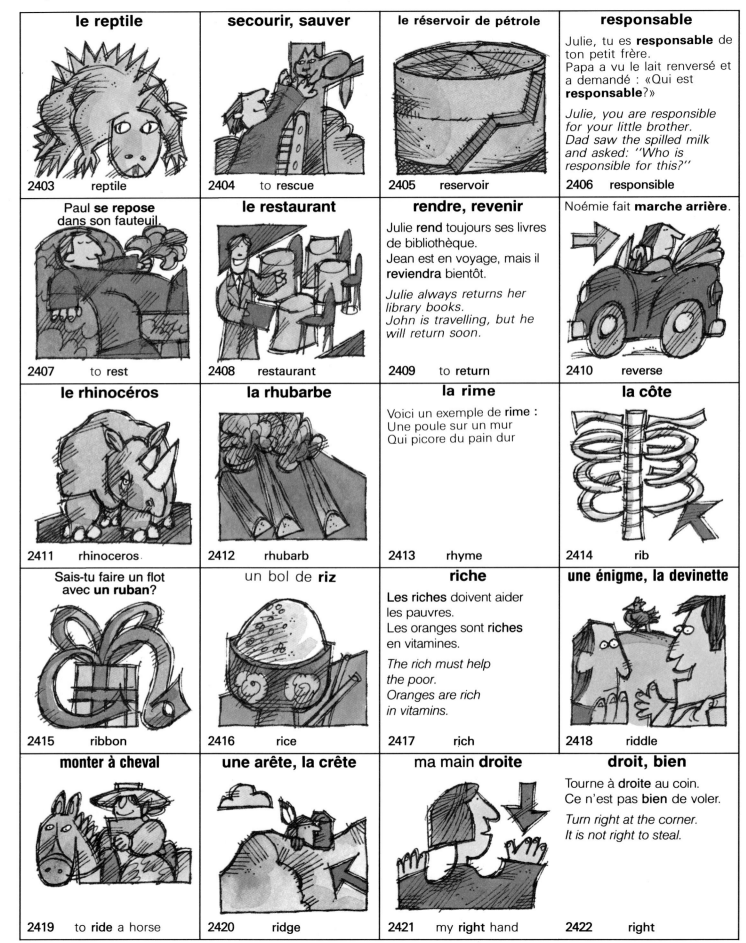

2403   reptile

secourir, sauver

2404   to rescue

le réservoir de pétrole

2405   reservoir

responsable

Julie, tu es **responsable** de ton petit frère.
Papa a vu le lait renversé et a demandé : «Qui est **responsable**?»

Julie, you are responsible for your little brother.
Dad saw the spilled milk and asked: "Who is responsible for this?"

2406   responsible

Paul **se repose** dans son fauteuil.

2407   to rest

le restaurant

2408   restaurant

rendre, revenir

Julie **rend** toujours ses livres de bibliothèque.
Jean est en voyage, mais il **reviendra** bientôt.

Julie always returns her library books.
John is travelling, but he will return soon.

2409   to return

Noémie fait **marche arrière**.

2410   reverse

---

le rhinocéros

2411   rhinoceros

la rhubarbe

2412   rhubarb

la rime

Voici un exemple de **rime** :
Une poule sur un mur
Qui picore du pain dur

2413   rhyme

la côte

2414   rib

Sais-tu faire un flot avec **un ruban**?

2415   ribbon

un bol de **riz**

2416   rice

riche

Les riches doivent aider les pauvres.
Les oranges sont **riches** en vitamines.

The rich must help the poor.
Oranges are rich in vitamins.

2417   rich

une énigme, la devinette

2418   riddle

---

monter à cheval

2419   to **ride** a horse

une arête, la crête

2420   ridge

ma main **droite**

2421   my **right** hand

droit, bien

Tourne à **droite** au coin.
Ce n'est pas **bien** de voler.

Turn right at the corner.
It is not right to steal.

2422   right

droitier	la couenne	la bague	L'oncle Pierre **sonne** à la porte.
2423 right-handed	2424 rind	2425 ring	2426 to ring

la patinoire	Papa **rince** la vaisselle.	une émeute	Il **a déchiré** son pantalon.
2427 rink	2428 to rinse	2429 riot	2430 to rip

La pomme est **mûre**.	l'ondulation, la ride	Le soleil **se lève**.	le risque
			Le météorologiste a dit qu'il y avait **un risque** de gelée. Sois prudent! Ne prends pas de **risques**! *The weatherman said there was a risk of frost. Be careful! Do not take any risks!*
2431 ripe	2432 ripple	2433 The sun rises.	2434 risk

des rivaux	**La rivière** serpente.	**La route** sinue.	Le lion **rugit**.
2435 rivals	2436 river	2437 road	2438 to roar

Le rôti sort du four.	le voleur	le rouge-gorge	le rocher
2439 roast	2440 robber	2441 robin	2442 rock

balancer, bercer	**la fusée**	**le fauteuil à bascule**	**la canne à pêche**
2443 to rock	2444 rocket	2445 rocking chair	2446 rod
le rouleau de papier	**rouler**	**le patin à roulettes**	**le rouleau à pâtisserie**
2447 roll	2448 to roll	2449 roller skate	2450 rolling pin
Le toit est fait de tuiles.	**la chambre, la pièce**	Le coq **se perche** pour la nuit.	**la racine**
2451 roof	2452 room	2453 to roost	2454 root
la corde	**La rose** a des épines.	**le romarin**	Mélanie a les joues **roses**.
2455 rope	2456 rose	2457 rosemary	2458 rosy
La pomme est **pourrie**.	**râpeux, rugueux**	Le bouton est **rond**.	**une rangée** de 4 boutons
2459 rotten apple	2460 rough	2461 round	2462 4 buttons in a **row**

Elle **rame** plus vite que Luc.	un habit **royal**	Le pneu et la balle sont en **caoutchouc**.	**les déchets, les détritus**
2463 to row	2464 royal	2465 rubber	2466 rubbish
Le rubis est une pierre rouge.	**le gouvernail**	Il est **malpoli**.	le terrain **accidenté**
2467 ruby	2468 rudder	2469 He is rude.	2470 rugged terrain
les ruines d'un ancien château	**la règle, le règne** Maman et Papa décident **des règles** de conduite à la maison. Certains pays sont sous **le règne** d'un roi. *Mother and Father make the rules in this house.* *Some countries are under the rule of a king.*	**Le souverain** règne.	J'entends **un grondement**.
2471 ruin	2472 rule	2473 ruler	2474 I hear a rumble.
courir	**se sauver**	**écraser**	**s'épuiser, arriver au bout de ses forces**
2475 to run	2476 to run away	2477 to run over	2478 to run out of energy
Elle se **précipite** pour attraper l'autobus.	Le robot est couvert de **rouille**.	**une ornière**	**Le seigle** pousse dans les champs.
2479 to rush	2480 rust	2481 rut	2482 rye

le sac de farine

2483 sack

La vérité est un principe **sacré**.

2484 Truth is a **sacred** principle.

triste

2485 sad

la selle

2486 saddle

Qu'est-ce qu'il y a dans **le coffre-fort**?

2487 safe

Le vent gonfle **la voile**.

2488 sail

la planche à voile

2489 sailboard

Le voilier vogue sur l'eau.

2490 sailboat/sailing boat*

le marin

2491 sailor

la salade

2492 salad

les soldes

2493 sale

le saumon

2494 salmon

le sel et le poivre

2495 salt

saluer

2496 to salute

pareil, identique

2497 same

le sable

2498 sand

la sandale

2499 sandal

Julie s'est préparé **un sandwich**.

2500 sandwich

la sève de l'érable

2501 sap

la sardine

2502 sardine

Le satellite tourne autour de la terre.

2503 satellite

une robe de **satin**

2504 satin dress

samedi

Le samedi, Julie ne va pas à l'école et peut jouer.

Julie can play on Saturday because she does not go to school.

2505 Saturday

la sauce

2506 sauce/gravy*

la saucisse

2507 sausage

J'**économise** mon argent.

2508 I **save** my money.

La scie a des dents.

2509 saw

la sciure

2511 sawdust

Je **dis** ce que je pense.

2512 I **say** what I think.

L'artiste est allongé sur son **échafaudage**.

2513 scaffolding

scier du bois

2510 to saw

échauder, ébouillanter

2514 to scald

La balance a deux plateaux.

2515 scale

la pétoncle, la coquille Saint-Jacques

2516 scallop

le cuir chevelu

2517 scalp

l'homme à **la cicatrice**

2518 scar

Elle trouve un malin plaisir à l'**effrayer**.

2519 to scare

Un épouvantail sert à effrayer les oiseaux.

2520 scarecrow

une écharpe bien chaude

2521 scarf

écarlate

2522   scarlet

la scène d'un crime

2523   scene of a crime

le paysage

2524   scenery

l'érudition, la bourse d'études

2525   scholarship

une école de village

2526   school

la goélette

2527   schooner

les ciseaux

2528   scissors

écoper, ramasser

2529   to scoop

le scooter

2530   scooter

Le papier est **roussi** par la flamme.

2531   scorched paper

marquer un but

2532   to score

le scout

2533   scout

des bouts de papier

2534   scraps of paper

une éraflure, une égratignure

2535   scrape

le grattoir, la gratte

2536   scraper

la griffure

2537   scratch

la moustiquaire

2538   screen

la vis

2539   screw

le tournevis

2540   screwdriver

frotter, récurer

2541   to scrub

Le sculpteur taille la pierre.

2542   sculptor

un hippocampe

2543   seahorse

la mer Adriatique

2544   Adriatic **sea**

la mouette, le goéland

2545   seagull

le phoque

2546   seal

la couture

2547   seam

Que **cherche**-t-il dans l'herbe?

2548   to **search**

le projecteur

2549   searchlight

les saisons

Les quatre **saisons** de l'année sont le printemps, l'été, l'automne et l'hiver.

The four seasons are spring, summer, autumn and winter.

2550   seasons

le siège

2551   seat

Julie a mis sa **ceinture** de sécurité.

2552   seatbelt

une algue

2553   seaweed

le second

2554   second

J'ai **un secret**.

2555   I have a **secret.**

voir

2556   to **see**

la bascule, la balance

2557   see-saw

De **la graine** naît la plante.

2558   seed

Il **semble** mort mais il ne l'est peut-être pas.

2559   It **seems** to be dead.

saisir

2560   to **seize**

Tu es **égoïste**, Marcel!

2561   You are **selfish.**

Marie vend des fruits.

2562　to sell

le demi-cercle

2563　semicircle

envoyer, expédier

2564　to send

une peau sensible

2565　sensitive skin

la phrase, la peine

Est-ce que tu sais faire **une phrase**?
Le voleur a été condamné à **une peine** de prison.

Can you make a sentence?
The robber received a prison sentence.

2566　sentence

la sentinelle

2567　sentry

Septembre est le neuvième mois de l'année.

2568　September

servir un repas

2569　to serve

sept

2570　seven

le septième

2571　seventh

plusieurs

2572　several

Elle **coud** avec du fil et une aiguille.

2573　to sew

la machine à coudre

2574　sewing machine

usé, élimé

2575　shabby

la cabane

2576　shack

une ombre

2577　shadow

un chien **à longs poils**

2578　shaggy

secouer

2579　to shake

une eau **peu profonde**

2580　shallow water

Maman se lave les cheveux avec du **shampooing**.

2581　shampoo

Nous pouvons **partager**.
2582   to share

Crois-tu que **le requin** apprend à voler?
2583   shark

tranchant, aiguisé
2584   sharp

Un affiloir sert à aiguiser.
2585   knife sharpener

fracasser, briser en éclats
2588   to shatter

se raser
2589   to shave

les cisailles
2590   shears

une affûteuse à patins
2586   skate sharpener

le fourreau
2591   sheath

Julie compte **des moutons** pour s'endormir
2592   sheep

le drap du lit
2593   sheet

le taille-crayons
2587   pencil sharpener

une étagère
2594   shelf

la coquille, le coquillage
2595   shell

L'insecte a trouvé **un abri**.
2596   shelter

Le berger. garde les moutons.
2597   shepherd

Le bouclier protège le guerrier.
2598   shield

le devant de la jambe
2599   shin

Le soleil **brille** de tous ses rayons.
2600   to shine

le bardeau
2601   shingle

Le zona est une maladie.

2602   shingles

Les diamants de la couronne sont **brillants**.

2603   shiny

le bateau, le navire

2604   ship

Robinson a fait **naufrage**.

2605   shipwreck

la chemise

2606   shirt

frissonner, grelotter

2607   to shiver

le choc

2608   shock

les chaussures, les souliers

2609   shoes

Est-ce que tu sais nouer tes **lacets**?

2610   shoelace

le cordonnier

2611   shoemaker

tirer

2612   to shoot

le magasin, la boutique

2613   shop

le marchand, le commerçant

2614   shopkeeper

la vitrine

2615   shop window

le rivage

2616   shore

petit, court

2617   short

un short

2618   shorts

une épaule

2619   shoulder

crier

2620   to shout

Il ne faut pas **pousser** les gens.

2621   to shove

la pelle pour enlever la neige	**montrer**	**parader, se pavaner**	Il a fini par **se montrer**.
2622 shovel	2623 to show	2624 to show off	2625 to show up/appear*
Julien prend **une douche**.	**pousser des cris aigus**	**la crevette**	Comme sa chemise **a rétréci**!
2626 shower	2627 to shriek	2628 shrimp	2629 to shrink
un arbuste	**battre, mélanger** les cartes	La nuit, on ferme **les volets**.	**timide**
2630 shrub	2631 shuffle	2632 shutters	2633 shy
malade	**le côté sans fenêtres**	Julie marche toujours sur **le trottoir**.	**soupirer** de fatigue, de tristesse
2634 sick	2635 side	2636 sidewalk/pavement*	2637 to sigh
la pancarte	**signaler**	**la signature**	**silencieux** Julie n'est pas souvent **silencieuse**. Une nuit **silencieuse** est une nuit tranquille. *Julie is not silent very often.* *A silent night is* *a quiet night.*
2638 sign	2639 to signal	2640 signature	2641 silent

le rebord de la fenêtre

2642　　sill

idiot, stupide

Sébastien pense que Julie
est complètement **idiote**.
Julie pense que Sébastien
fait des choses **stupides**.

*Sébastien thinks Julie
is silly.
Julie thinks Sébastien does
silly things.*

2643　　silly

L'argent est un métal précieux.

2644　　silver

simple

C'est la vérité pure et
simple.
Il y a une solution très
simple.

*That is the truth, pure and
simple.
There is a very simple
solution.*

2645　　simple

chanter

2646　　to sing

singulier

«Un» est **singulier**.
«Plusieurs» est pluriel.

*''One'' is singular.
''Several'' is plural.*

2647　　singular

un évier de cuisine

2648　　sink

Au secours! Le bateau coule.

2649　　to sink

**siroter, boire
à petites gorgées**

2650　　to sip

la sirène

2651　　siren

Paule est la sœur de Laurent.

2652　　sister

être assis

2653　　to sit

six

2654　　six

le sixième

2655　　sixth

Est-ce que c'est ma taille?

2656　　size

patiner

2657　　to skate

la planche à roulettes

2658　　skateboard

Un squelette dans le placard?!

2659　　skeleton

L'artiste dessine.

2660　　to sketch

les skis

2661　　skis

skier	Horace a presque **dérapé**.	**la peau**	**sauter** à la corde
2662 to ski	2663 to skid	2664 skin	2665 to skip
Le capitaine tient le gouvernail.	**la jupe**	**le crâne**	**Le ciel** est nuageux.
2666 skipper/captain*	2667 skirt	2668 skull	2669 sky
une alouette	**le gratte-ciel**	Barnabé **a claqué** la porte.	un plancher **incliné**
2670 skylark	2671 skyscraper	2672 to slam	2673 slanting floor
donner une claque, gifler	**taillader, sabrer**	**une ardoise**	**La luge** dévale la pente.
2674 to slap	2675 to slash	2676 slate	2677 sled/sleigh*
Zorro **dort** avec son sabre.	**le sac de couchage, le duvet**	Paul se sent tout **somnolent**.	**la neige fondante**
2678 to sleep	2679 sleeping bag	2680 sleepy	2681 sleet

la manche

2682   sleeve

le toboggan

2683   slide

L'une est mince, l'autre est grosse.

2684   slim

Le ver a un corps visqueux.

2685   slimy

Il a le bras en écharpe.

2686   sling

la fronde, le lance-pierre

2687   slingshot/catapult*

glisser

2688   to slip

la pantoufle

2689   slipper

glissant

2690   slippery

Comme il est malpropre!

2691   slob

La pente de la montagne est rude.

2692   slope

la fente

2693   slot

Il ne faut pas se tenir voûté.

2694   to slouch

ralentir

Ralentis Papa! Tu roules trop vite!
La voiture ralentit au coin de la rue.

Slow down, Dad! You are going too fast.
The car slows down at the corner.

2695   to slow down

la neige à demi-fondue

2696   slush

L'un est petit, l'autre est grand.

2697   small

intelligent, élégant

Julie a fait quelque chose de très **intelligent**.
Elle porte une robe très **élégante**.

Julie did a very smart thing.
because she passed her exam.
She is wearing a very smart dress.

2698   smart/clever*

écraser, démolir

2699   to smash

barbouiller, salir

2700   to smear

Comme cette fleur sent bon!

2701   to smell

La mouffette a une odeur **nauséabonde!**

2702   smelly

fumer

2703   to smoke

lisse, en douceur

La glace sur laquelle Julie patine est bien **lisse**.
Un bon pilote sait atterrir **en douceur**.

The ice Julie is skating on is very smooth.
A good pilot makes smooth landings.

2704   smooth

Noémie aime **goûter** entre les repas.

2705   to have a snack

un escargot

2706   snail

le serpent

2707   snake

se casser avec un bruit sec

2708   to snap

les espadrilles de sport

2709   sneakers/trainers*

La poussière l'a fait **éternuer**.

2710   to sneeze

le masque et **le tube**

2711   snorkel

La neige tombe du ciel.

2712   snow

le flocon de neige

2713   snowflake

les raquettes

2714   snowshoes

Lave-toi les mains avec du **savon!**

2715   soap

le foot-ball

2716   soccer

la chaussette

2717   sock

la prise de courant

2718   socket

le sofa, le canapé

2719   sofa/couch*

Sacha a la fourrure **douce**.

2720   soft

le soldat

2721   soldier

la sole

2722   sole

Elle résout un problème.

2723   She solves the problem.

faire la culbute

2724   to somersault

le père et le fils

2725   son

le chant, la chanson

2726   song

bientôt

Il fera bientôt nuit.
Julie sera bientôt de retour
à la maison.

Soon it will be dark.
Julie will be home soon.

2727   soon

Le sorcier jette un
mauvais sort.

2728   sorcerer

Mon bras est **douloureux.**

2729   My arm is sore.

L'oseille a un goût acide.

2730   sorrel

Milou est absolument **navré.**

2731   sorry

Il **trie** les bons des mauvais.

2732   to sort

la soupe

2733   soup

Le citron est **acide.**

2734   sour

le sud

2735   south

La truie est la mère
des porcelets.

2736   sow

semer

2737   to sow

le vaisseau spatial

2738   spaceship

La bêche sert à jardiner.

2739   spade

donner la fessée

2740   to spank

la roue de secours

2741   spare tire/tyre*

une étincelle	Ses bagues **étincellent** au soleil.	**le moineau**	Quelle langue **parlent**-ils?
2742 spark	2743 to sparkle	2744 sparrow	2745 to speak
la lance	La tortue a du mal à **accélérer**.	Alice va **épeler** son prénom.	**dépenser** de l'argent
2746 spear	2747 to speed up	2748 to spell	2749 to spend
la sphère	**épicé**	**Une araignée** tisse sa toile.	**le piquant**
2750 sphere	2751 spicy	2752 spider	2753 spike
renverser, répandre	La toupie **tourne**.	**les épinards**	**la colonne vertébrale**
2754 to spill	2755 to spin	2756 spinach	2757 spine
la spirale	**la flèche** de l'église	Ce n'est pas poli de **cracher**!	**éclabousser**
2758 spiral	2759 spire	2760 to spit	2761 to splash

un éclat de bois

2762　splinter

Les fruits sont gâtés.

2763　spoiled/rotten* fruit

une éponge

2764　sponge

la bobine de fil

2765　spool/reel*

la cuillère

2766　spoon

D'où vient cette vilaine **tache?**

2767　spot

le bec de la théière

2768　spout

se faire une entorse

2769　to sprain

vaporiser

2770　to spray

étaler

2771　to spread

le ressort

2772　spring

Le printemps est enfin arrivé!

2773　spring

saupoudrer

2775　to sprinkle

sprinter, faire une course de vitesse

2776　to sprint

le sapin, une épinette

2777　spruce

La source coule vite.

2774　spring

le carré

2778　square

la courge, la gourde

2779　squash

s'accroupir

2780　to squat

Julie **serre** son ami dans ses bras.

2781　to squeeze

le calmar	**un écureuil**	**faire gicler**	**une écurie** à chevaux
2782 squid	2783 squirrel	2784 to squirt	2785 stable
la scène du théâtre	**la tache**	Où mène **l'escalier?**	**un piquet** en bois
2786 stage	2787 stain	2788 staircase	2789 wooden stake

rassis

Je n'aime pas le pain **rassis**, je préfère le pain frais.

I do not like stale bread, I prefer fresh bread.

2790   stale bread

la branche de céleri	**Un étalon** est un cheval mâle.	**le timbre**
2791 celery stalk	2792 stallion	2793 stamp

être debout, se tenir debout	**une étoile**	Julie **regarde fixement** devant elle.	**un étourneau**
2794 to stand	2795 star	2796 to stare	2797 starling

faire démarrer une voiture	**mourir de faim**

mourir de faim

Quand Julie rentre de l'école, elle crie: «Je **meurs de faim!**» Elle est affamée, mais elle ne va pas vraiment **mourir de faim.**

When Julie comes back from school, she always shouts: ''I'm starving.'' She is very hungry, but she will not really starve.

2798 to start a car	2799 to starve	**la station-service**	**la gare**
		2800 gas/petrol* station	2801 train/railway* station

la statue

2802   statue

Médor! **Reste** là!

2803   Stay there!

un steak, un bifteck

2804   steak

Le cambrioleur **vole**.

2805   to steal

la vapeur

2806   steam

Les couteaux sont en **acier**.

2807   Kinves are made of **steel**.

escarpé, à pic

2808   steep

le bœuf

2809   steer/bullock*

la tige de la rose

2811   stem

la marche

2812   step

Elle **a marché dans** la flaque.

2813   to step in

conduire, diriger

2810   to steer

Papa a préparé **un ragoût**.

2815   stew

la baguette

2816   stick

sortir une minute

2814   to step out

Didier a les mains **collantes**.

2817   sticky

raide, dur

Oncle Jean a la jambe **raide**.
Cette brosse à dents est trop **dure**.

Uncle Jean has a stiff leg.
This toothbrush is too stiff.

2818   stiff

Une abeille l'**a piquée**.

2819   to sting

la piqûre

2820   sting

sentir très mauvais

2821   to stink

Remue avant de goûter!

2822   to stir

les bas

2823   stockings

charger une chaudière

2824   to stoke

un estomac

2825   stomach

le caillou, ia pierre

2826   stone

L'araignée descend vers **le tabouret.**

2827   stool

Elle **se baisse** pour ramasser la balle.

2828   to stoop/bend down*

un arrêt, le stop

2829   stop

le magasin

2832   store/shop*

la cigogne

2833   stork

un orage, la tempête

2834   storm

Il **arrête** le train.

2830   He **stops** the train.

Tante Annie lit **une histoire.**

2835   story

la cuisinière

2836   stove/cooker*

droit, rectiligne

2837   straight

L'avion a fait **une escale.**

2831   to stop over

filtrer

2838   to strain

forcer, peiner

2839   to strain

Quel **étrange** animal!

2840   strange

Jo s'est trop approché. Le singe va l'**étrangler.**

2841   to strangle

la bretelle
2842   strap

Est-ce que tu aimes boire avec **une paille**?
2843   straw

la fraise
2844   strawberry

le cours d'eau, la rivière
2845   stream

la banderole, le fanion
2846   streamer/pennant*

La rue est déserte.
2847   street

le réverbère
2848   street light/lamp*

étirer
2849   to stretch

le brancard, la civière
2850   stretcher

la grève
Les ouvriers sont en **grève** parce qu'ils veulent une augmentation.
The workers are on strike for more money.
2851   strike

Il ne faut pas **frapper** les gens.
2852   to strike

La ficelle est enroulée sur la bobine.
2853   string

une serviette à **rayures**
2854   stripe

Il est très **fort**.
2855   strong

un étudiant
2856   student

Il **étudie** sagement.
2857   to study

un animal **rembourré**
2858   a stuffed animal

la souche
2859   stump

Le sous-marin navigue sous l'eau.
2860   submarine

soustraire
2861   to subtract

sucer

2862   to suck

---

soudain, brusquement

Il a **soudain** commencé
à pleuvoir.
Amélie est **brusquement**
partie.

Suddenly, it began to rain.
Amélie left suddenly.

2863   suddenly

Ne mange pas trop de **sucre**!

2864   sugar

Louis porte **un costume**.

2865   suit

---

la valise

2866   suitcase

---

un été au bord de la mer

2867   summer

---

le soleil

2868   sun

---

dimanche

Dimanche est l'un des
jours de la semaine.
Tous les **dimanches**,
Maman fait un gâteau.

Sunday is one of the days
of the week.
Every Sunday, Mother
bakes a cake.

2869   Sunday

Le cadran solaire
indique l'heure.

2870   sundial

Le tournesol fait face au soleil.

2871   sunflower

---

le lever du soleil

2872   sunrise

---

le coucher du soleil

2873   sunset

Aude fait les courses
au **supermarché**.

2874   supermarket

---

le dîner, le souper

2875   supper/dinner*

---

sûr, certain

Je suis **sûr** qu'il fera
beau demain.
C'est un moyen **certain**
de gagner.

I am sure it will be
nice tomorrow.
That is a sure way to win.

2876   sure

---

la surface

2877   surface

---

le chirurgien

2878   surgeon

---

le nom de famille

Mon prénom est Julie, mon
nom de famille est Dubois.

My first name is Julie and
my surname is Dubois.

2879   surname

---

la surprise-partie

2880   surprise party

Ne tirez pas! Je **me rends**.

2881   to surrender

entourer, encercler

2882   to surround

Les bretelles retiennent son pantalon.

2883   suspenders/braces*

avaler

2884   to swallow

Le cygne est majestueux.

2885   swan

échanger, troquer

2886   to swap

un essaim d'abeilles en colère

2887   swarm

Il **transpire** à grosses gouttes.

2888   to sweat

le chandail, le tricot

2889   sweater/sweatshirt*

balayer

2890   to sweep

sucré

2891   sweet

Heureusement, l'auto **a fait un écart.**

2892   to swerve

André sait bien **nager**.

2893   to swim

la balançoire

2894   swing

se balancer

2895   to swing

un interrupteur

2896   switch

allumer, éteindre

Allume la lumière, s'il te plaît.
Il vaut mieux **éteindre** la télévision.

Switch on the light, please. It is best to switch off the television.

2897   to switch

s'abattre, fondre sur une proie

2898   to swoop

une épée

2899   sword

le sycomore

2900   sycamore

Le sirop d'érable est bon avec des gaufres!

2901   syrup

La tasse est sur **la table**.

2902 table

La nappe a des carreaux bleus et blancs.

2903 tablecloth

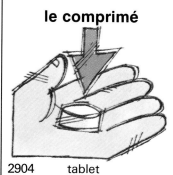

le comprimé

2904 tablet

la pointe, la punaise

2905 tack

s'attaquer à, plaquer

Julie doit **s'attaquer à** ce problème au plus vite.
Alain **a plaqué** Yves au sol durant la partie de rugby.

Julie must tackle that problem as soon as possible.
Alain tackled Yves during the rugby match.

2906 to tackle

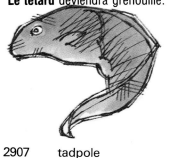

Le têtard deviendra grenouille.

2907 tadpole

Il a **la queue** touffue.

2908 tail

prendre

2910 to take

démonter

2911 to take apart

emporter

2912 to take away

rapporter

2913 to take back

enlever

2914 to take off

décoller

2915 to take off

sortir

2916 to take out

le repas à emporter

2917 take-out/take-away*

Le tailleur fait des vêtements.

2909 tailor

le récit, une histoire

2918 tale

le talent

Sylvie a beaucoup de **talent** pour la danse.
Pour bien danser, il faut du **talent** et de l'effort.

Sylvie has a great talent for dancing.
Dance requires both talent and hard work.

2919 talent

parler

2920 to talk

grand, haut	le tambourin	dompté, apprivoisé	Elle a **un** beau **bronzage**.
2921 tall	2922 tambourine	2923 tame	2924 tan
la mandarine	Le fil est tout **emmêlé!**	**le réservoir, la citerne**	le pétrolier, le navire-citerne
2925 tangerine	2926 tangled	2927 tank	2928 tanker
Le robinet fuit goutte à goutte.	**le ruban adhésif**	**fixer avec du ruban adhésif**	**le magnétophone** et la cassette
2929 tap	2930 tape	2931 to tape	2932 tape recorder
le goudron	en plein dans **la cible**	**l'estragon**	**la tarte, la tartelette**
2933 tar	2934 target	2935 tarragon	2936 tart
la tâche, le travail	**Goûte** et dis-moi si c'est bon!	**succulent, savoureux**	**le taxi**
2937 task	2938 to taste	C'était un repas **succulent**. La tarte était **savoureuse**. *This was a tasty meal.* *The tart was very tasty.* 2939 tasty	2940 taxi

une tasse de **thé**

2941   a cup of tea

Mademoiselle Blanche **enseigne** le calcul.

2942   to teach

C'est notre **institutrice**.

2943   teacher

une équipe inséparable

2944   team

la **théière**

2945   teapot

la **larme**

2946   tear

déchirer

2947   to tear

Il ne faut jamais **arracher** les pages!

2948   to tear out

le **télégramme**

2949   telegram

le **téléphone**

2950   telephone

Margot aime **téléphoner** à ses amis.

2951   to telephone

Le téléscope est braqué vers le ciel.

2952   telescope

La télévision, c'est la télé ou la TV.

2953   television

Elle lui **dit** ce qu'elle pense.

2954   to tell

le caractère

Christophe a mauvais **caractère**.
Il n'arrive pas à rester calme.

Christophe has a bad temper.
He cannot control his temper.

2955   temper

Le thermomètre marque **la température**.

2956   temperature

dix pommes

2957   ten apples

la raquette et la balle de **tennis**

2958   tennis racquet and ball

la chaussure de **tennis**

2959   tennis shoe

Julie a dormi sous **la tente.**

2960   tent

le dixième escargot	**le terminal** de l'ordinateur	**essayer** l'eau	Elle le **remercie** de tout cœur.
2961 tenth	2962 terminal	2963 to **test** the water	2964 to **thank**
dégeler	**le théâtre**	La balle est **là!**	**Le thermomètre** est gradué.
2965 to thaw	2966 theater/theatre*	2967 there	2968 thermometer
Cet arbre a un tronc **épais**.	**Le voleur** porte un masque.	**la cuisse**	**le dé à coudre**
2969 thick	2970 thief	2971 thigh	2972 thimble
Le tronc de cet arbre est **mince**.	**la chose** Une personne, ce n'est pas **une chose**. Julie dit beaucoup de **choses** amusantes. *A person is not a thing. Julie says many funny things.*	**penser**	**le troisième** escargot
2973 thin	2974 thing	2975 to **think**	2976 third
Il **a soif**, il est **assoiffé**.	Attention! **Le chardon** est piquant.	**une épine**	**le fil**
2977 thirsty	2978 thistle	2979 thorn	2980 thread

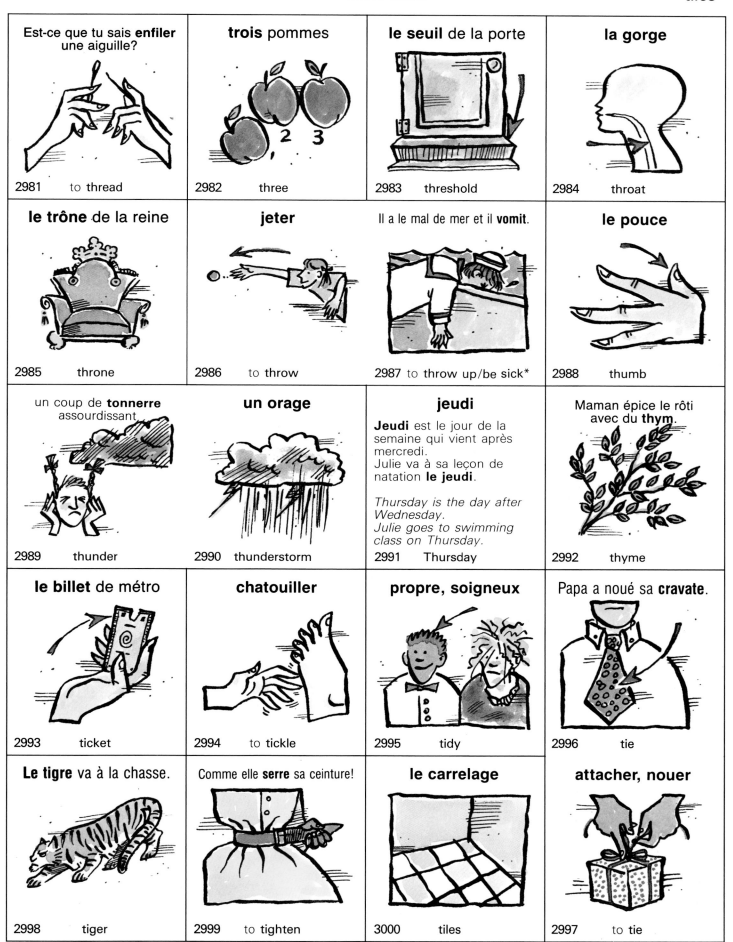

Est-ce que tu sais enfiler une aiguille?

2981   to thread

trois pommes

2982   three

le seuil de la porte

2983   threshold

la gorge

2984   throat

le trône de la reine

2985   throne

jeter

2986   to throw

Il a le mal de mer et il **vomit.**

2987   to throw up/be sick*

le pouce

2988   thumb

un coup de **tonnerre** assourdissant

2989   thunder

un orage

2990   thunderstorm

jeudi

Jeudi est le jour de la semaine qui vient après mercredi.
Julie va à sa leçon de natation **le jeudi.**

Thursday is the day after Wednesday.
Julie goes to swimming class on Thursday.

2991   Thursday

Maman épice le rôti avec du **thym.**

2992   thyme

le billet de métro

2993   ticket

chatouiller

2994   to tickle

propre, soigneux

2995   tidy

Papa a noué sa **cravate.**

2996   tie

Le tigre va à la chasse.

2998   tiger

Comme elle **serre** sa ceinture!

2999   to tighten

le carrelage

3000   tiles

attacher, nouer

2997   to tie

Le bateau **penche** dangereusement.

3001   to tilt

Quelle **heure** est-il?

3002   What **time** is it?

minuscule

3003   tiny

Le bateau **a chaviré**.

3004   to tip

marcher sur la pointe des pieds

3006   tiptoe

Est-ce que **le pneu** est assez gonflé?

3007   tire/tyre*

fatigué, las

3008   tired

donner un pourboire

3005   to tip

Le crapaud vit près de la mare.

3009   toad

le toast, le pain grillé

3010   toast

le grille-pain

3011   toaster

aujourd'hui

L'école commence **aujourd'hui**.
Aujourd'hui, Julie se lève tôt pour préparer son petit déjeuner.

School starts today.
Today Julie gets up early to make her breakfast.

3012   today

les orteils

3013   toes

Nous sommes assis **ensemble**.

3014   We are sitting **together**.

les toilettes

3015   toilet

la tomate

3016   tomato

la tombe

3017   tomb

demain

Demain suit aujourd'hui.
Demain, Julie va voir les dinosaures au musée.

Today is followed by tomorrow.
Tomorrow, Julie is going to see the dinosaurs at the museum.

3018   tomorrow

les pinces

3019   tongs

Voyons! Ne tire pas **la langue**!

3020   tongue

Il pèse une tonne.

3021   It weighs a **ton**.

les amygdales

3022   tonsils

les outils du bricoleur

3023   tools

Elle a de belles dents.

3024   tooth

le mal de dents

3025   toothache

la brosse à dents

3026   toothbrush

le dentifrice

3027   toothpaste

le sommet, le haut

3028   top

tomber, dégringoler

3030   to topple

le flambeau olympique

3031   torch

La tornade balaie tout sur son passage.

3032   tornado

La toupie tourne sur elle-même.

3029   top

le torrent

3033   torrent

La tortue a une carapace.

3034   tortoise

lancer, jeter

3035   to toss

toucher

3036   to touch

Je suis dur.

3037   I am **tough**.

Le camion remorque l'auto.

3038   to tow

Julie s'essuie avec la serviette.

3039   towel

la tour la plus haute au monde

3040   tower

la ville	Ramasse tes **jouets** s'il te plaît!	**tracer**	Le train suit **la voie** ferrée.
3041 town	3042 toys	3043 to trace	3044 track
le tracteur	**échanger, faire des affaires**	**La circulation** est dense.	**les feux de circulation**
3045 tractor	3046 to trade	3047 traffic	3048 traffic light
Il est sur **la bonne piste**.	Qu'est-ce qu'il y a dans **la remorque**?	**le train**	Elle **dresse** son chien.
3049 trail	3050 trailer	3051 train	3052 to train
le vagabond	Il ne faut pas **piétiner** les fleurs!	**le tremplin**	Le verre que tient la maman de Julie est **transparent**.
3053 tramp	3054 to trample	3055 trampoline	3056 transparent
transporter	**le camion-plateau, le fardier**	La souris se méfie du **piège**.	**le trapèze**
3057 to transport	3058 transporter/lorry*	3059 trap	3060 trapeze

Tante Annie **voyage** en train.
3061   to travel

Ne renverse pas **le plateau**!
3062   tray

la bande de roulement du pneu
3063   tread

le trésor
3064   treasure

un arbre
3065   tree

Judith **tremble** de peur.
3066   to tremble

la tranchée
3067   trench

le procès
3068   trial

Le triangle a trois côtés.
3069   triangle

le tour, le truc
3070   trick

couler goutte à goutte
3071   to trickle

Le tricycle a trois roues.
3072   tricycle

la détente, la gachette du pistolet
3073   trigger

Le coiffeur lui **égalise** les cheveux.
3074   to trim

un voyage court
3075   a short trip

trébucher
3076   to trip

le trolleybus
3077   trolley bus

Le poulain aime **trotter** et galoper.
3078   to trot

une auge à cochons
3079   trough

le pantalon
3080   trousers

la truite

3081   trout

la truelle du maçon

3082   trowel

le camion

3083   truck/lorry*

vrai, véritable

Est-ce que c'est **vrai** que Julie a traversé l'océan à la nage? C'est un **véritable** ami.

Is it true that Julie swam across the ocean? He is a true friend.

3084   true

Est-ce que tu sais jouer de **la trompette?**

3085   trumpet

la malle, le coffre

3086   trunk

le tronc

3087   trunk

la trompe
de Jumbo l'éléphant

3088   trunk

Ils se **font confiance**.

3089   to trust

Diane, dis-moi **la vérité!**

3090   truth

essayer

Essaie de te souvenir où tu ranges tes affaires! **Essaie** une fois de plus!

Try to remember where you put your things! You must try again.

3091   to try

la baignoire

3092   tub

---

le tube

3093   tube

mardi

Mardi est le jour de la semaine qui suit le lundi. **Le mardi**, Julie a une leçon de piano.

Tuesday is the day after Monday. On Tuesdays, Julie has a piano lesson.

3094   Tuesday

Chacun **tire** de son côté.

3095   to tug

la tulipe

3096   tulip

---

culbuter, tomber

3097   to tumble

Comme il fait noir dans **le tunnel!**

3098   tunnel

la dinde

3099   turkey

tourner

3100   to turn

éteindre

3101   to **turn off**

allumer

3102   to **turn on**

devenir, tourner

Quelle jolie petite fille elle **est devenue**.
Les choses **ont** bien **tourné**.

What a pretty girl she turned out to be!
Things turned out well.

3103   to **turn out**

tourner, retourner

3104   to **turn over**

le navet

3105   turnip

le tourne-disque

3106   turntable

turquoise

3107   turquoise

Le guetteur est dans **la tourelle**.

3108   turret

la tortue

3109   turtle

Les défenses de l'éléphant sont en ivoire.

3110   tusk

la pince à épiler

3111   tweezers

deux fois

Julie est allée au zoo **deux fois**.
Caroline a **deux fois** plus de livres que moi.

Julie has been to the zoo twice.
Caroline has twice as many books as I.

3112   twice

la brindille

3113   twig

Les jumeaux sont identiques.

3114   twins

Les étoiles scintillent.

3115   Stars twinkle.

tourner, tournoyer

3116   to **twirl**

tordre, tortiller

3117   to **twist**

deux

3118   two

écrire à la machine, dactylographier

3119   to **type**

la machine à écrire

3120   typewriter

Elle est **laide** mais si gentille.

3121   ugly

le parapluie

3122   umbrella

un oncle

Mon **oncle** est le frère de ma mère.
Mon autre **oncle** est le frère de mon père.

My uncle is my mother's brother.
My other uncle is my father's brother.

3123   uncle

sous, moins de

Julie se cache **sous** les couvertures.
Les enfants de **moins de** 5 ans ne peuvent pas y aller.

Julie is hiding under the covers.
Children under 5 cannot go.

3124   under

comprendre

3125   to understand

les sous-vêtements

3126   underwear

se déshabiller

3127   to undress

triste, malheureux

3128   unhappy

La licorne n'existe que dans les fables.

3129   unicorn

L'oncle Richard porte **un uniforme**.

3130   uniform

Fabienne est diplômée de **l'université**.

3131   university

Qu'est-ce que le camion **décharge**?

3132   to unload

déverrouiller

3133   to unlock

déballer

3134   to unwrap

debout

3135   upright

à l'envers

3136   upside-down

Maman **utilise** du poivre pour faire la cuisine.

3137   to use

Elle **a tout utilisé** le poivre.

3138   to use up

Ce couteau de poche est très **utile**.

3139   useful

Vivent **les vacances**!

3140   vacation/holiday*

la vapeur

3141   vapor/vapour*

Anatole **vernit** le bois pour le protéger.

3142   to varnish

Julie a fait cadeau d'**un vase** à sa maman.

3143   vase

une côtelette de **veau**

3144   veal

les légumes

3145   vegetable

le véhicule

3146   vehicle

---

le voile, la voilette

3147   veil

la veine

3148   vein

le venin

Le venin est le poison des serpents vénimeux. Certains insectes ont aussi du **venin**.

Venom is the poison of poisonous snakes. Some insects also have venom.

3149   venom

Une ligne droite, de haut en bas, est **verticale**.

3150   vertical

---

très

Julie pense que son petit frère est **très** malin. La soupe sera prête **très** bientôt.

Julie thinks her little brother is very clever. Very soon the soup will be ready.

3151   very

le gilet

3152   vest/waistcoat*

Le vétérinaire soigne les animaux.

3153   veterinarian/veterinary surgeon*

la victime du crime

3154   victim

---

le magnétoscope

3155   video recorder

Il ne faut pas jouer avec **une bande vidéo**.

3156   video tape

la vue

Quelle belle **vue** nous avons du sommet de la montagne! Chacun de nous a son point de **vue**.

What a wonderful view from the top of the mountain! We each have our own point of view.

3157   view

le village

3158   village

le bandit, le gredin

3159 villain

Les raisins sont les fruits de **la vigne**.

3160 vine

Du **vinaigre** sur les frites!

3161 vinegar

Grand-mère aime le parfum de **la violette**.

3162 violet

le violon

3163 violin

Il faut **un visa** pour aller à l'étranger.

3164 visa

visible

Il y a beaucoup de nuages ce soir et les étoiles sont à peine **visibles**.
On ne peut pas voir du tout un homme **invisible**.

There are many clouds tonight and the stars are barely visible.
An invisible man cannot be seen.

3165 visible

visiter, rendre visite

3166 to visit

la visière

3167 visor

le vocabulaire

Julie a **un vocabulaire** riche; elle sait beaucoup de mots. Ce dictionnaire t'aidera à enrichir ton **vocabulaire**.

Julie has a good vocabulary; she knows many words. This dictionary will help increase your vocabulary.

3168 vocabulary

la voix

3169 voice

Le volcan crache de la lave.

3170 volcano

le volley-ball

3171 volleyball

volontaire, bénévole

3172 volunteer

Il a mangé quelque chose de mauvais; il **vomit**.

3173 to vomit

voter aux élections

3174 to vote

Un électeur vote.

3175 voter

la voyelle

A, E, I, O, U et Y sont **les seules voyelles** de l'alphabet.

A, E, I, O, U and Y are the only vowels in the alphabet.

3176 vowel

le voyage

3177 voyage

le vautour

3178 vulture

marcher dans l'eau, patauger

3179   to wade

la gaufre

3180   waffle

Le cheval tire **la charrette**.

3181   wagon/cart*

gémir, pleurer

3182   to wail

Lucie a **la taille** fine.

3183   waist

Carole **attend** l'autobus.

3184   to wait

réveiller

3185   to wake

Elle **marche** à grands pas.

3186   to walk

le mur

3187   wall

le portefeuille

3188   wallet

la noix

3189   walnut

le morse

3190   walrus

la baguette magique

3191   wand

se promener sans but, errer

3192   to wander

vouloir

Papa **veut** que Julie l'aide
à faire la vaisselle.
Elle **veut** bien l'**aider**, mais
il n'y a pas d'eau.

*Dad wants Julie to help him
wash the dishes.
She wants to help him but
there is no water.*

3193   to want

Julie a horreur de
la guerre.

3194   war

la garde-robe

3195   wardrobe

Cet **entrepôt** contient
beaucoup de marchandises.

3196   warehouse

un pull-over bien **chaud**

3197   warm

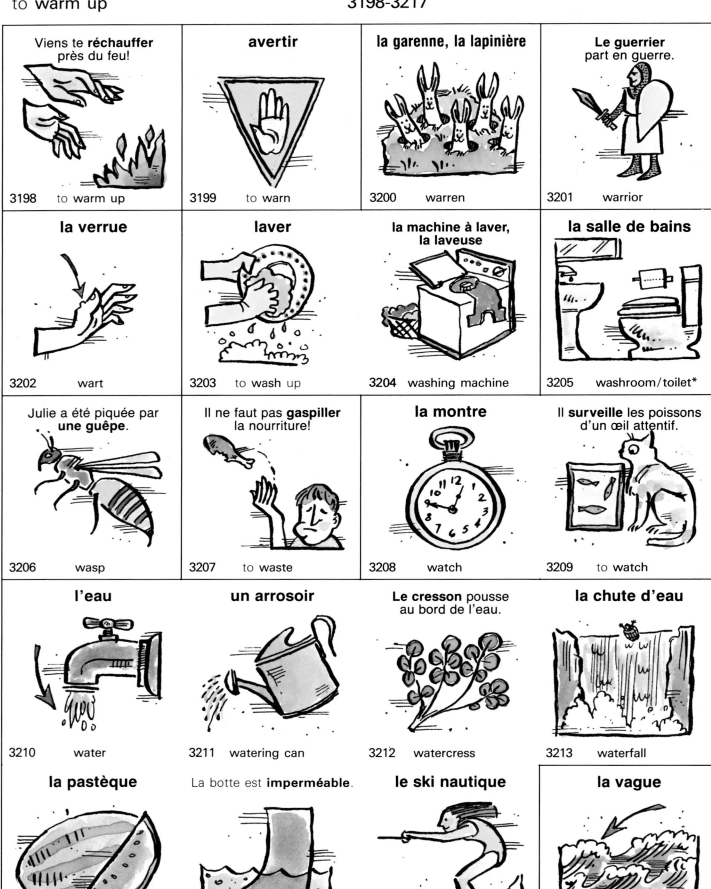

Viens te **réchauffer** près du feu!

3198   to warm up

avertir

3199   to warn

la garenne, la lapinière

3200   warren

Le guerrier part en guerre.

3201   warrior

la verrue

3202   wart

laver

3203   to wash up

la machine à laver, la laveuse

3204   washing machine

la salle de bains

3205   washroom/toilet*

Julie a été piquée par **une guêpe**.

3206   wasp

Il ne faut pas **gaspiller** la nourriture!

3207   to waste

la montre

3208   watch

Il **surveille** les poissons d'un œil attentif.

3209   to watch

l'eau

3210   water

un arrosoir

3211   watering can

Le cresson pousse au bord de l'eau.

3212   watercress

la chute d'eau

3213   waterfall

la pastèque

3214   watermelon

La botte est **imperméable**.

3215   waterproof

le ski nautique

3216   waterskiing

la vague

3217   wave

faire signe

3218 to wave

Elle a les cheveux **ondulés.**

3219 wavy

La cire de la bougie coule.

3220 wax

L'un est **faible,** l'autre est fort.

3221 weak

une arme dangereuse

3222 weapon

Il **porte** des vêtements chauds.

3223 to wear

la belette

3224 weasel

Quel **temps** fait-il?

3225 weather

tisser

3226 to weave

un pied **palmé**

3227 web foot

le mariage

3228 wedding

le coin, le morceau triangulaire

3229 wedge

mercredi

Mercredi est le jour de la semaine qui vient après mardi.
Le mercredi, Julie sort les poubelles.

Wednesday is the day after Tuesday.
On Wednesdays, Julie takes out the garbage.

3230 Wednesday

Le jardin est envahi par **les mauvaises herbes.**

3231 weed

La semaine a sept jours.

3232 week

la fin de semaine, le week-end

La fin de semaine est faite du samedi et du dimanche. Tante Lucie nous rendra visite ce **week-end.**

Saturday and Sunday make a weekend.
Aunt Lucie will visit us this weekend.

3233 weekend

Il **pleure** parce qu'il est triste.

3234 to weep

peser

3235 to weigh

Ce dessin est **étrange, bizarre.**

3236 weird

Hélène **souhaite la bienvenue** à son ami.

3237 to welcome

Ne tombe pas dans le puits!

3238   well

Je me sens bien.

3239   I feel well.

L'ouest est opposé à l'est.

3240   west

humide, mouillé

3241   wet

la baleine

3243   whale

le quai

3244   wharf

quoi, que

Quoi? Que dis-tu?
Que veux-tu pour le petit déjeuner?

What? What did you say? What do you want for breakfast?

3245   what

mouiller

3242   to wet

Le blé donne de la farine.

3246   wheat

la roue

3247   wheel

la brouette

3248   wheelbarrow

la chaise roulante

3249   wheelchair

quand

Quand tante Émilie viendra-t-elle nous voir?
Quand elle aura ses vacances.

When is Aunt Émilie coming to see us? When she takes her holidays.

3250   when

où

Nous sommes perdus et maman n'a pas la moindre idée **où** nous sommes. Je sais **où** c'est, mais je n'arrive pas à le retrouver.

We are lost and Mother has no idea where we are. I know where it is, but I cannot find it.

3251   where

Il ne sait pas lequel choisir.

3252   which one

pleurnicher

3253   to whine

le fouet

3254   whip

un engoulevent

3255   whippoorwill

Le fouet sert à battre les œufs et la crème.

3256   whisk

la moustache du chat

3257   whisker

Qu'est-ce qu'elle lui **chuchote** à l'oreille?	**le sifflet**	**siffler**	**blanc**
3258 to **whisper**	3259 **whistle**	3260 to **whistle**	3261 **white**
Qui y va?	**pourquoi** Je veux savoir **pourquoi** Julie a pris ma cravate. **Pourquoi** ne peut-elle pas s'en souvenir? *I want to know why Julie took my tie.* *Why can she not remember?*	**La mèche** brûle lentement.	**mauvais, méchant**
3262 **Who** is going?	3263 **why**	3264 **wick**	3265 **wicked**
large	Madame Arthaud est **la femme** de Monsieur Arthaud.	Le lion est un animal **sauvage**.	**Le saule** a de longues branches.
3266 **wide**	3267 **wife**	3268 The lion is a **wild** animal.	3269 **willow**
Les fleurs **se fanent** quand elles manquent d'eau.	**rusé, astucieux**	**gagner**	**grimacer de douleur**
3270 to **wilt**	3271 **wily**	3272 to **win**	3273 to **wince**
Le vent souffle avec rage.	**remonter**	**le blouson, le coupe-vent**	**Le moulin à vent** a des ailes.
3274 **wind**	3275 to **wind**	3276 **windbreaker**	3277 **windmill**

la fenêtre

3278 window

le pare-brise

3279 windshield/windscreen*

Le vin est réservé aux adultes.

3280 wine

une aile

3281 wing

cligner de l'œil

3282 to wink

Est-ce que tu aimes **l'hiver**?

3283 winter

Essuie bien, s'il te plaît.

3284 to wipe

Les oiseaux sont perchés sur **le fil**.

3285 wire

sage, prudent

Grand-père est un vieil homme **sage**.
Julie, crois-tu qu'il est **prudent** de te promener seule en forêt?

Grandfather is a wise old man.
Julie, do you think it is wise to walk in the forest alone?

3286 wise

faire **un vœu**

3287 to make a wish

la sorcière

3288 witch

le magicien

3289 wizard

le loup

3290 wolf

la femme

3291 woman

se demander

3292 to wonder

un **merveilleux** feu d'artifice

3293 wonderful

le bois

3294 wood

Le pivert pique le tronc de l'arbre.

3295 woodpecker

Ils se promènent dans **les bois**.

3296 woods

le travail du bois

3297 woodwork

Elle tricote avec de **la laine**.

3298   wool

Quel drôle de **mot**!

GLÜRP

3299   word

le travail

3300   work

Elle **travaille** au jardin.

3301   to work

un atelier

3303   workshop

le monde

3304   world

Le ver se tortille.

3305   worm

faire des exercices physiques

3302   to work out

s'inquiéter

3306   to worry

la blessure

3307   wound

emballer, envelopper

3308   to wrap

la guirlande, la couronne de fleurs

3309   wreath

une épave

3310   wreck

le roitelet

3311   wren

Ils **luttent** férocement.

3312   to wrestle

tordre le linge

3313   to wring

le poignet

3314   wrist

la montre-bracelet

3315   wristwatch

écrire

3316   to write

mal, mauvais

C'est **mal** de tricher
et de voler.
Je pense que notre autobus
va dans le **mauvais** sens.

*It is wrong to cheat and
to lie.
I think our bus is going the
wrong way.*

3317   wrong

les rayons X, la radiographie
3318   X-ray

le xylophone
3319   xylophone

le yacht
3320   yacht

la cour
3321   yard/garden*

Est-ce qu'il **bâille** d'ennui ou de sommeil?
3322   to yawn

un an, une année
3323   year

hurler, crier
3324   to yell

jaune
3325   yellow

oui
C'est **oui**, c'est non, ou c'est peut-être? Si tu dis **oui**, tu dois être sûr.

Is it yes, is it no, or is it maybe? If you say yes, you had better be sure.

3326   yes

hier
Hier, Julie a été malade parce qu'elle avait mangé trop de crème glacée. Qu'est-ce que tu as fait **hier**?

Yesterday, Julie was sick from eating too much ice cream. What did you do yesterday?

3327   yesterday

Isabelle doit **céder** le passage.
3328   to yield/give way*

le jaune d'œuf
3329   yolk

jeune et vieux
3330   young

le **zèbre** qu'a dessiné Julie
3331   zebra

zéro
3332   zero

la fermeture éclair
3333   zipper/zip*

le zoo
3334   zoo

filer à toute allure
3335   to zoom

La courgette est le dernier mot de Julie.
3336   zucchini/courgette*

a

à 117
à longs poils 1091
à part 78
à réaction 1485, 1486
abaisser 1699
abandonner 839
abattre (s') 2898
abeille (une) 216
abîmé 724
aboyer 174
abri (un) 2596
abricot (un) 87
absent 4
accélérateur (un) 5
accélérer 2747
accent (un) 6
accident (un) 7
accidenté 2470
accordéon (un) 8
accorder 1184
accrocher 1261
accroupir (s') 2780
accumuler 1341
accuser 9
acheter 398
acide (un) 12, 2734
acier (un) 2807
acrobate (un, une) 14
additionner 16
adieu 956
adorer 19
adresse (une) 17
adroit 1258
adulte (un, une) 20, 1221
aéroglisseur (un) 1390
aéroport (un) 40
affaire (une) 1750
affamé 2352
affiche (une) 2211
affiloir (un) 2585
affreux 136
affûteuse (une) 2586
Afrique 25
âge (un) 30
agenouiller (s') 1541
agent de police (un)
    615, 2185
agente de police (une)
    2186

agile 31
agneau (un) 1561
agréable 2157
agriculteur (un) 958
agripper 1207
aider 1308
aigle (un) 858
aiglefin (un) 1235
aiguille (une) 1890
aiguisé 2584
ail (un) 1107
aile (une) 3281
aile d'auto (une) 976
ailleurs (d') 239
aimable 1176
aimant (un) 1713
aimer 1644, 1695, 1696
air (un) 36
aire de jeux (une) 2155
airelle (une) 1394
aisselle (une) 98
album de photos (un)
    43
algue (une) 2553
alimenter 972
allée (une) 41
alléger 1640
aller 1157
alligator (un) 48
allongé 1930
allumer 1638, 2897,
    3102
allumette (une) 1748
alouette (une) 1577,
    2670
alphabet (un) 54
aluminium (un) 58
amande (une) 49
amasser 1341
ambulance (une) 60
amende (une) 991
amer 258
ami (un) 1073
amiral (un) 18
ampoule (une) 278,
    1639
amusant 1089
amuser (s') 1085
amygdale (une) 3022
an (un) 3323
ananas (un) 2126

ancien 63
ancre (une) 62
âne (un) 803
ange de mer (un) 1826
angle (un) 64
anguille (une) 875
animal (un) 66
animal familier (un)
    2092
animer 1668
année (une) 3323
anniversaire (un) 254
annoncer 68
annuler 410
Antarctique (l') 72
antilope (une) 73
août 126
apercevoir (s') 2361
aplatir 1020
apparaître 82
appareil-photo (un) 414
appartenir 231
appât (un) 148
appeler 409
applaudir 83, 537
apporter 351
apprécier 898
apprendre 1602
apprivoisé 2923
approcher 86
appui-tête (un) 1289
appuyer 2233, 2261
après 26
après-midi (un, une)
    27
aquarium (un) 90
arachide (une) 2060
araignée (une) 2752
arbitre (un) 2382
arbre (un) 3065
arbre à feuilles
    persistantes (un) 913
arbuste (un) 391, 2630
arc (un) 322
arc-en-ciel (un) 2338
arche (une) 91
architecte (un, une) 92
Arctique (l') 93
ardoise (une) 2676
arête (une) 2420
argent (l') 1824, 2644

argent liquide (l') 454
argile (une) 540
arme (une) 3222
armé de piquants 2238
armoire (une) 401
armure (une) 97
arracher 2948
arranger 100
arrêt (un) 2829
arrêt d'autobus (un)
    390
arrêter 101, 2830
arrêter un instant (s')
    2050
arrière 1335
arriver 102, 1265
arrosoir (un) 3211
artichaut (un) 104
articulation (une) 1494,
    1548
artiste (un, une) 105
as (un) 10
ascenseur (un) 886
Asie (l') 109
asperge (une) 112
aspirine (une) 113
assassiner 1858
assez 900
assiette (une) 2151
assoiffer (être) 2977
asticot (un) 1710
astronaute (un, une)
    115
astronome (un, une)
    116
astucieux 3271
atelier (un) 3303
athlète (un, une) 118
atlas (un) 119
atmosphère (une) 120
atome (un) 121
âtre (un) 1002
attacher 122, 250, 960,
    2997
attaque (une) 2334
attaquer à (s') 2906
atteindre 2357
attendre 924, 3184
attendre à (s') 924
attention (faire) 123

d

glissant 2690
glisser 1153, 2688
glorifier 2224
goéland (le) 2545
goélette (la) 2527
golf (le) 1166
golfe (le) 1229
gomme (la) 1232
gonfler 923
gorge (la) 2984
gorille (le) 1172
goudron (le) 2135, 2933
gourde (la) 2779
goûter 2705, 2938
goutte (la) 835
gouvernail (le) 1306, 2468
gouvernement (le) 1174
gouverner 1173
grain (le) 1178, 1515
grain de beauté (le) 1821
graine (la) 1515, 2558
graisse (la) 1195
gramme (le) 1179, 1525
grand 245, 1576, 2921
grand immeuble (le) 1329
grand magasin (le) 749
grand vent (le) 1095
grand-mère (la) 1182
grand-père (le) 1181
grande route (la) 1331
grande sturnelle (la) 1757
grandir 1219
grange (la) 177
granit (le) 1183
graphique (le) 494, 1187
gras 961
grassouillet 2168
gratte (la) 2536
gratte-ciel (le) 2671
grattoir (le) 2536
gravier (le) 1192
gravité (la) 1193
gredin (le) 3159
grêle (la) 1236
grelotter 2607

grenade (la) 2190
grenier (le) 124, 1681
grenouille (la) 1075
grève (la) 2851
griffure (la) 2537
grignoter 1906
grille-pain (le) 3011
griller 1203
grimacer de douleur 3273
grimper 544, 1160
grippe (la) 1033
gris 1202
grogner 1220
grondement (le) 2474
gronder 1220
gros 961
gros caillou (le) 319
groseille (la) 703, 1170
grossier 564
grotte (la) 466
groupe (le) 1218
grue (la) 657, 658
guêpe (la) 3206
guérir 2375
guérir (être) 699, 1290
guerre (la) 3194
guerrier (le) 3201
gui (le) 1810
guide (le) 1598
guider 1225
guirlande (la) 3309
guitare (la) 1228

h

habiller (s') 822
habiter 1439
habitude (une) 1234
hache (la) 138
hacher 525, 1206
hachette (la) 1278
haie (la) 1300
haleine (une) 341
haleter 2013
halloween (une) 1243
hamac (le) 1248
hameçon (un) 1007, 1366

hamster (le) 1249
hanche (la) 1336
handicap (le) 1254
hangar (le) 1262
hanté 1280
hardi 1058
hareng (le) 1320
hareng doux (le) 1533
haricot (le) 204
haricot vert (le) 1199
harmonica (un) 1271
harnais (le) 1272
harpe (la) 1273
haut (le) 3028
haut-parleur (le) 1693
haut 1328
haute voix (à) 53
hélice (une) 2262
hélicoptère (un) 1303
hémisphère (un) 1311
hennir 1892
heptagone (un) 1313
herbe (une) 1188, 1314
hérisson (le) 1301
hermétique 38
héroïne (une) 1319
héros (le) 1318
hésiter 1321
hêtre (un) 217
heure (une) 1387, 3002
heureux 1266
heurter 659
hexagone (un) 1322
hiberner 1323
hibou (le) 1981
hier 3327
hippocampe (un) 2543
hippopotame (un) 1337
histoire (une) 1338, 2835, 2918
hiver (un) 3283
hochet (le) 2349
hockey (le) 1344
homard (le) 1675
homme (un) 1723
honnête 1357
honneur (un) 1362
hôpital (un) 1382
hoqueter (1324)
horizon (un) 1372
horizontal 1373

hôtel (un) 1386
houe (la) 1347
houx (le) 1353
huile (une) 1942
huit 878
huitième (le, la) 879
huître (une) 1985
humeur (une) 1830, 1831
humide 725, 1819, 3241
hurler 1392, 3324
hutte (la) 1408
hymne (un) 1411
iceberg (un) 1415
ici 1316
idée (une) 1418
idiot 1420, 2643
igloo (un) 1423
île (une) 1467
illuminer 1426
illustration (une) 1427
imperméable (un) 2339, 3215
important 1428
imprimer 2245
impuissant 1309
incendie (un) 271
incliné 2673
inculper 492
index (un) 1432
indication (une) 557
indice (un) 557
indigo 1433
indiquer 2176
infecte 1060
infection (une) 1436
initiale (une) 1440
injection (une) 1441
inondation (une) 1028
inquiéter (s') 3306
inscrire (s') 2387
insecte (un) 372, 1444
insecte nuisible (un) 2090
insigne (un) 146
insister 1446
insouciant 441
inspecter 1447
inspecteur (un) 1448
institutrice (une) 2943

ouvert 1952
ouvre-boîte (un) 418
ouvre-bouteille (un)
  317
ouvrir 1953
oval 1973
oxygène (l') 1984

p

pacane (la) 2066
pagaie (la) 1990
pagayer 1991
page (la) 1993
paille (la) 2843
pain (le) 336, 1673
pain d'épice (le) 1141
pain grillé (le) 3010
pair 911
paire (la) 2002
paître 1194
paix (la) 2055
palais (le) 2003
pâle 2004
palefrenier (le) 1212
palette (la) 2005
palier (le) 1568
palmé 3227
palourde (la) 535
pamplemousse (le)
  1186
panais (le) 2030
pancarte (la) 2638
panda (le) 2009
panier (le) 188
panneau d'affichage
  (le) 248
pansement (le) 163
pantalon (le) 2015,
  3080
panthère (la) 2014
pantoufle (la) 2689
paon (le) 2057
papaye (la) 2016
papier (le) 2017
papillon (le) 396
paquebot (le) 1654
parachute (le) 2018
parade (la) 2019
parader 2624

paradis (le) 1298
paralyser 2021
parapluie (le) 3122
paratonnerre (le) 1643
parc (le) 2024
parce que 211
pardessus (le) 1976
pardonner 919, 1053
pare-brise (le) 3279
pare-chocs (le) 381
pareil 2497
parents (les) 2023
parenté (la) 2392
paresseux 1596
parfum (le) 1021, 2086
parka (la) 2026
parlement (le) 2027
parler 2745, 2920
parmi 61
partager 2582
partenaire (le, la) 2032
particule (la) 2031
parti (être) 135
partie (la) 1747
partir 1157, 1606
pas (le) 1047
pas de mal 56
passage (le) 2036
passage pour piétons
  (le) 2071
passagère (la) 2037
passé (le) 2039
passe-temps (le) 1343,
  2042
passeport (le) 2038
passer 2034
passer voir 837
pastèque (la) 3214
patauger 3179
pâte (la) 807
pâte à modeler (la)
  2150
pâté de maisons (le)
  281
pâtes (les) 2040
patient (le) 2048
patient (être) 2047
patin à roulettes (le)
  2449
patiner 2657
patinoire (la) 2427

pâtisserie (la) 2043
patron (le) 314
patron de couture (le)
  2049
patte (la) 2052
pâturage (le) 2044
paume (la) 2006
pauvre 2195
pavaner (se) 2624
pavot (le) 2198
payant 2054
payer 2053
pays (le) 643
paysage (le) 2524
peau (la) 1325, 2664
pêche (la) 2056
pêcher 1006
pédale (la) 2068
pédale d'accélérateur
  (la) 1111
pédaler 2069
peigne (le) 584
peigner (se) 585
peindre 1998
peiner 2839
peintre (le) 2000
peinture (la) 1996, 2001
peinture fraîche (la)
  1997
peler 2072
pélican (le) 2073
pelle (la) 2622
pelouse (la) 1592
peluche (la) 1034
penché 676
pencher 1601, 3001
pendule (la) 547, 2076
péniche (la) 173
pensée (la) 2012
penser 2975
pentagone (le) 2079
pente (la) 2692
percer 310, 826, 2286
perceuse (la) 827
perche (la) 2083
percher (se) 2453
perchoir (le) 2084
perdre 1690
perdu (un peu) 611
père (le) 963
perle (la) 201, 2062

perroquet (le) 2028
persil (le) 2029
personne 1919
personne (la) 2089
pervenche (la) 2088
peser 3235
pétale (le) 2094
pétard (le) 1000
petit 2617, 2697
petit déjeuner (le) 340
petit-fils (le) 1180
petit 1666
pétoncle (le) 2516
pétrole (le) 1942
pétrolier (le) 2928
pétunia (le) 2095
peu 981
peu profond 2580
peuple (le) 2080
peuplier (le) 2197
peur (la) 24
peut-être 1753
phare (le) 1641
pharmacie (la) 2097
pharmacienne (la) 2096
phoque (le) 2546
photo (la) 2100
photographie (la) 2100
phrase (la) 2566
piaffer 2225
piano (le) 2101
pic (à) 2808
pic (le) 2058
picorer 2067
pie (la) 1716
pièce (la) 2045, 2452
pièce de monnaie (la)
  574
pied (le) 1044
piège (le) 3059
pierre (la) 2826
pierre précieuse (la)
  1117
piétiner 3054
piéton (le) 2070
piètre 2195
pieuvre (la) 1935
pigeon (le) 2114
pile électrique (la) 195
pilier (le) 2118, 2207
pilote (le) 2121